Oracle Certification Prep

Study Guide for

1Z0-055: Oracle Database 11g:

New Features for 9i OCPs

Matthew Morris

Study Guide for Oracle Database 11g: New Features for 9i OCPs (Exam 1Z0-055) Rev 1.1

ISBN-13: 978-1477499924
ISBN-10: 147749992X

Oracle Certification Prep

Table of Contents

What to Expect from the Test

The test consists of 84 multiple choice or multiple answer questions. The passing score listed on Oracle Education at this time is 61%. However, as with all OCP tests, they note it is subject to change. As is true of most upgrade certifications, 1Z0-055 deals primarily with concepts and facts. It is not an exam designed to verify your ability to use the database. Testing the ability to use features generally requires that an exam have a simulator to give the ability to enter commands or navigate a GUI.

When you sit to take the exam for 1Z0-055, you must be familiar with the major features that have been added or changed in the database between 9i and 11G. You must also know how any given change affects using or administering the database, and the steps required to enable, disable, or configure the new feature. You won't be programming PL/SQL statements or navigating a GUI interface during the test. What is primarily being determined is whether or not you are aware of the existence of the new features and the functionality they provide.

That's not to say that you won't be required to answer any questions on how to use some of the new features. However, for features that are particularly complex to implement, you are unlikely to see a question that requires you to know the complete implementation process. Put another way, if a new feature is invoked with a single command -- you're likely to need to know that command for the test. If a feature requires thirty lines of PL/SQL to execute, you're likely to be asked a question about what the feature does rather than how to do it.

What to Expect from this Study Guide

The guide will be covering a significant percentage of the changes that were made to the Oracle database between the Oracle 9i and Oracle 11G releases. Oracle Education has created a list of test objectives for this exam that is a compromise between the most important changes made and the number of topics that can be covered in a single test. For example, a number of the topics from the 10G to 11G upgrade exam are missing from the list for this test.

This book has been designed to hit the knowledge areas indicated on the list for this exam. The information presented in this book assumes that you are already familiar with the Oracle database as an administrator. The guide and the test are targeted for individuals who are Oracle Database 9i Administrator Certified Professionals. You should have already taken and passed several exams demonstrating your knowledge of the Oracle database.

This guide is intended as much as possible to present information that is likely to be on the test at the level it will be presented. As an example, for your career as an Oracle DBA, it would be <u>ideal</u> if you knew all of the PL/SQL procedures required to perform a SQL Performance Analyzer operation and could type them in freehand without referring to any manual. For the test, however, what is likely to be asked is the sequence of steps in analyzing SQL using SPA and possibly the names of the procedures used. The purpose of this guide is to help you pass the test and so will not go into exhaustive details about any of the new features.

Ideally in studying for any certification test, you should utilize multiple resources. One of those should be a source that provides the full details for using the new features. However, those tend to be hefty books that are hard enough to read through a single time. Read through them only once and you're liable to miss something important. This guide is small enough that you can read it several times before scheduling the test. Repetition will help to reinforce your knowledge and help prevent you from missing key facts that can lead to incorrect answers on the test.

Additional Study Resources

The companion website to this series is www.oraclecertificationprep.com. The site contains many additional resources that can be used to study for this exam (and others). From the entry page of the website, click on the 'Exams' button, and then select the link for this test. The Exam Details page contains links to the following information sources:

- Applicable Oracle documentation.
- Third-party books relevant to the exam.
- White papers and articles on Oracle Learning Library on topics covered in the exam.
- Articles on the Web that may be useful for the exam.

The website will never link to unauthorized content such as brain dumps or illegal content such as copyrighted material made available without the consent of the author. I cannot guarantee the accuracy of the content links. While I have located the data and scanned it to ensure that it is relevant to the given exam, I did not write it and have not proofread it from a technical standpoint. The material on the Oracle Learning Library is almost certain to be completely accurate and most of the other links come from highly popular Oracle support websites and are created by experienced Oracle professionals.

I recommend that you use more than one source of study materials whenever you are preparing for a certification. Reading information presented from multiple different viewpoints can help to give you a more complete picture of any given topic. The links on the website can help you to do this. Fully understanding the information covered in this certification is not just valuable so that getting a passing score is more likely – it will also help you in your career. I guarantee that in the long run, any knowledge you gain while studying for this certification will provide more benefit to you than any piece of paper or line on your resume.

Installation and Upgrade Enhancements

Install Oracle Database 11g

Changes to the OFA

The directory structure used in Oracle's installation process has been redesigned in 11G. The directory structure now centers around the ORACLE_BASE environment variable. Prior to 11G, setting this variable was optional and the only required environment variable was ORACLE_HOME. As of 11G, ORACLE_BASE is the only required parameter, and the ORACLE_HOME setting will be derived from ORACLE_BASE. The new structure streamlines how the installation is organized, and makes ongoing management easier. This feature improves manageability by making the directory structure more compliant with Optimal Flexible Architecture (OFA) specifications.

The default value for ORACLE_BASE is "/mount_point/app/oracle_software_owner". If you are installing as OS user oracle to the mount point u01, the default ORACLE_BASE would be: "/u01/app/oracle/". If the ORACLE_BASE environment variable is not set when prompted during the install process, the install will complete successfully, but when the database is started you'll receive an error in the alert log that ORACLE_BASE is not set in the environment.

Automatic Diagnostic Repository

The Automatic Diagnostic Repository (ADR) is a designated portion of the OFA directory structure for storing trace files and other diagnostic data. It provides a single location for all the serious errors encountered by the database and the data needed to diagnose and resolve them. The default ADR base directory is $ORACLE_BASE/diag. The default location can be changed with the use of the diagnostic_dest initialization parameter. The ADR structure is designed so that multiple database instances and other Oracle components such as Oracle Clusterware, Oracle OCI, Oracle Net, and more, can make use of the structure for storing diagnostic files. Each product has an ADR home using the syntax: $ORACLE_BASE /product_type/product_id/instance_id. For an Oracle database with a SID and database name of 'orcl11g', the ADR home would be $ORACLE_BASE /rdbms/orcl11g/orcl11g.

Flash Recovery Area

In Oracle 11G, the Flash Recovery Area is located immediately below the ORACLE_BASE: $ORACLE_BASE/flash_recovery_area.

Data Files

The Oracle data file directory is likewise located immediately beneath the $ORACLE_BASE: $ORACLE_BASE/oradata. Note that Oracle strongly recommends you use separate physical drives for the oradata and flash_recovery_area directories.

Changes to Installation Options & Components

New Components

- Oracle has added several database components to the installation process.
- Oracle Application Express is now installed by default with Oracle Database 11g. It was previously available as a separate Companion CD component.
- Oracle Configuration Manager is a new optional component during installation. It was previously named Customer Configuration Repository (CCR). Oracle Configuration Manager gathers and stores details relating to the configuration of Oracle software.
- Oracle Database Vault is a new optional component during database installation.
- Oracle Real Application Testing is installed by default with the Enterprise Edition installation type of Oracle Database 11g.
- Oracle SQL Developer is installed by default with template-based database installations, such as General Purpose/Transaction Processing, and Data Warehousing.
- Oracle Warehouse Builder is installed by default with Oracle Database 11g.

Other Changes

- Oracle HTTP Server is now available on a separate media.
- Oracle Ultra Search is now integrated with the Oracle Database.
- Oracle XML DB is no longer an optional feature.

Upgrade your database to Oracle Database 11g

Upgrade path

An upgrade to Oracle 11G, performed either manually via scripts or using the Database Upgrade Assistant can only directly upgrade databases of version 9.2.0.4 or higher. Databases prior to that version must go through an intermediate upgrade process that results in a database of 9.2.0.4 (or higher) before you can upgrade to 11G.

Manual upgrade to 11G

When performing a manual upgrade to Oracle 11G, there are five scripts that must be run for the upgrade process to complete successfully. It's important that you remember function of each and the order in which they get run. When upgrading a database, the very first step is to make sure that you have a good backup. After taking a backup, you'll shut the database down and issue a startup upgrade to open the database in upgrade mode. Upgrade mode disables system triggers and prepares the data dictionary for update.

Once the database is started in upgrade mode, you can begin running the scripts. The Pre-Upgrade information tool is called utlu111i.sql. This script is technically a precursor to the upgrade. It generates a report that contains required and recommended changes that you must make. You might need to increase the size of SYSAUX, change or remove parameters, among other actions. Once the information tool indicates the database is ready, you will run the 11G Upgrade script: catupgrd.sql. This is the script that will make the actual changes to the database structure to bring it to the 11G model. If the script is stopped or fails before completion, it can be re-run multiple times. At completion, the catupgrd.sql script will shut the database down. Once it has completed, you will restart the database in normal mode and run the Post Upgrade Status script: utlu111s.sql. This script verifies that all components have been upgraded to 11G. If some have not, you will need to run the catupgrd.sql script again. Note that the Pre-Upgrade and Post-Upgrade scripts have very similar names. You need to remember which is which for the test. After the status script shows all components have been upgraded to 11G, you must run the Post upgrade actions script: catuppst.sql. This script is new with 11G and performs numerous upgrade tasks that don't require the database to be in upgrade mode. Simultaneously with catuppst.sql (or before or after), you may run the utlrp.sql script. This script recompiles and revalidates any database objects shown as INVALID in the Post-Upgrade Status script.

While it's not explicitly listed as a test component, I'll note that the script catdwgrd.sql is what you would use if you wanted to downgrade your database back to the pre-upgrade version.

Database Upgrade Assistant (DBUA)
It's also possible (and in most cases preferable) to upgrade to Oracle 11G using the Database Upgrade Assistant or DBUA. There's much less to remember (and much less to be tested on) with DBUA. You should know that DBUA can upgrade database and ASM instances simultaneously, whereas manual upgrades must upgrade them separately. DBUA is also somewhat faster at the end as it can recompile objects in parallel on multi-CPU systems.

The following enhancements have been added to DBUA:

- For single-instance databases, Oracle DBUA configuration utility enables you to upgrade from Oracle Database XE to Oracle Database 11g.
- You can move datafiles to ASM, OFS, or other storage devices, such as Storage Area Networks (SAN) and Network Area Storage (NAS), as part of the upgrade.
- The directory that you specify when you are prompted for ORACLE_BASE by Oracle Universal Installer is stored in the Oracle home inventory. DBUA uses this value to derive the default database locations and the DIAGNOSTIC_DEST parameter.
- The command line option AUTOEXTEND facilitates auto extending of the data files as a part of the upgrade. This option autoextends the data files during the upgrade and turns the autoextend back to its original settings after the upgrade.

COMPATIBLE parameter
The COMPATIBLE parameter of the Oracle database affects a great deal of its behavior. Much of the 11G functionality will be disabled if the parameter is lower than the database version. The default value for 11G Release 1 is 11.1.0. The default value for Release 2 is 11.2.0. For both R1 and R2, the minimum allowed value is 10.0.0.

Use online patching

Traditional vs. Online Patches

Prior to 11G, all patches contained .o (object) files and/or .a (archive) libraries. Installing them required a relink of the RDBMS binary and therefore meant the database had to be shut down before the patch could be applied. With 11G, some patches are available as online patches. These contain .so files, which are dynamic/shared libraries, and they do not require a relink of the RDBMS binary. Because a relink is not needed, online patches can be applied or rolled back while the database instance is running. This simplifies administration, because no downtime is needed. It also means that installing or de-installing Online Patches is faster -- potentially taking just a few seconds. Online patches will be installed using the opatch utility.

Benefits

The benefits of online patches include the following:

- No downtime is required
- They persist across shutdowns
- They allow rolling patches in RAC
- They have a fast installation

Downsides

There are few downsides to online patches:

- They require more memory
- Online patching isn't available on all platforms
- Not all patches are available as hot patches

Storage Enhancements

Create and maintain bigfile tablespaces

A bigfile tablespace is a tablespace with a single, but very large datafile. It allows you to have a tablespace with a datafile larger than is normally allowed for a single file. Bigfile tablespaces are supported only for locally managed tablespaces with automatic segment space management. The exceptions to this are locally managed undo tablespaces, temporary tablespaces, and the SYSTEM tablespace. There are several benefits of bigfile tablespaces:

- A bigfile tablespace with 32K blocks can contain a 128 terabyte datafile. Because there is an upper limit on the total number of datafiles in an Oracle database, one using bigfile tablespaces can greatly increase the storage limit.
- With fewer datafiles needed, the DB_FILES initialization parameter and MAXDATAFILES parameter can be lowered. This reduces the amount of SGA space required for datafile information and the size of the control file.
- Database management is simplified because the syntax for the ALTER TABLESPACE statement lets you perform operations on tablespaces, rather than the underlying individual datafiles.

Creating a Bigfile Tablespace

To create a bigfile tablespace, specify the BIGFILE keyword of the CREATE TABLESPACE statement. Oracle Database automatically creates a locally managed tablespace with automatic segment space management. The EXTENT MANAGEMENT clause defaults to LOCAL and the SEGMENT SPACE MANAGEMENT defaults to AUTO. If you specify EXTENT MANAGEMENT DICTIONARY or SEGMENT SPACE MANAGEMENT MANUAL, the database will return an error. The remainder of the CREATE TABLESPACE statement remains the same, with the exception that you can only specify a single datafile.

```
CREATE BIGFILE TABLESPACE bigftbs
DATAFILE '/u01/oradata/oraprod/bigftbs01.dbf' SIZE 500G;
```

The SIZE can be specified in kilobytes (K), megabytes (M), gigabytes (G), or terabytes (T). It is possible to set the default tablespace type to BIGFILE at database creation. If this is done, there is no need specify the keyword BIGFILE in the CREATE TABLESPACE statement. In that case, if you want to create a traditional tablespace, you must specify SMALLFILE in the CREATE TABLESPACE statement.

Altering a Bigfile Tablespace

Two clauses of the ALTER TABLESPACE statement support datafile transparency when you are using bigfile tablespaces:

- **RESIZE** -- The RESIZE clause lets you resize the single datafile in a bigfile tablespace to an absolute size, without referring to the datafile. For example:

  ```
  ALTER TABLESPACE bigftbs RESIZE 800G;
  ```

- **AUTOEXTEND** -- With a bigfile tablespace, you can use the AUTOEXTEND clause outside of the ADD DATAFILE clause. For example:

  ```
  ALTER TABLESPACE bigftbs AUTOEXTEND ON NEXT 50G;
  ```

An error is raised if you specify an ADD DATAFILE clause for a bigfile tablespace.

Rename tablespaces

In 10G, Oracle added the RENAME clause to the ALTER TABLESPACE command. This clause will allow you to rename a tablespace if the tablespace and all of its data files are online. The database COMPATIBLE parameter must be set to 10.0.0 or greater. You can rename both permanent and temporary tablespaces, with the exception of SYSTEM and SYSAUX. If a tablespace is read only, then the data file headers are not updated to reflect the new name. A message in the alert log will indicate this. If a tablespace has been designated as the undo tablespace for any instance in a RAC environment, and a server parameter file was used at database startup, then the value of UNDO_TABLESPACE for that instance is changed in the server parameter file. If a single-instance database is using a parameter file (pfile) instead of a spfile, a message in the alert log will indicate that the pfile value must be changed.

```
ALTER TABLESPACE tbs01 RENAME TO tbs02;
```

Create a default permanent tablespace

In 10G, Oracle introduced the concept of a default permanent tablespace. Prior to this, if a newly created user account was not explicitly given a default tablespace, any objects they created would be placed in the SYSTEM tablespace. The CREATE DATABASE and ALTER DATABASE commands have had a new DEFAULT TABLESPACE clause added to them. It's possible to set the default permanent at database creation or at any time afterwards. When a default permanent tablespace is created for the database, Oracle assigns to this tablespace any non-SYSTEM users for whom you do not explicitly specify a different permanent tablespace. The tablespace specified must already have been created.

```
ALTER DATABASE DEFAULT TABLESPACE users;
```

Describe Automatic Storage Management (ASM)

Oracle Automatic Storage Management (ASM) is storage solution for Oracle Database files. It acts as a volume manager to provide a file system for the exclusive use of the database. When using ASM, partitioned disks are assigned to ASM with specifications for striping and mirroring. The ASM instance will then manage the disk space and distributing the load to optimize performance. ASM provides several benefits over using standard datafiles:

- Simplifies operations such as creating databases and managing disk space
- Distributes data across physical disks to provide uniform performance
- Rebalances data automatically after storage configuration changes

The logical storage elements of an Oracle ASM instance are:

- **ASM Disks** -- A storage device that is provisioned to an Oracle ASM disk group. It can be a physical disk or partition, a Logical Unit Number (LUN) from a storage array, a logical volume, or a network-attached file.
- **ASM Disk Groups** -- A collection of Oracle ASM disks managed as a logical unit.
- **ASM Files** -- A file stored in an Oracle ASM disk group. The database can store data files, control files, online redo log files, and other types of files as Oracle ASM files.
- **ASM Extents** -- The raw storage used to hold the contents of an Oracle ASM file. An ASM file consists of one or more file extents and an ASM extent consists of one or more ASM allocation units.
- **ASM Allocation Units** -- The fundamental unit of allocation within a disk group.
- **ASM Instances** -- A special Oracle instance that manages Oracle ASM disks. They manage the metadata of the disk group and provide file layout information to the database instances.

Two new background processes support ASM instances: RBAL and ORBn.

- **RBAL** -- Coordinates the disk activity for disk groups on an ASM instance
- **ORBn** -- Performs the actual extent movement between disks in the disk groups.

For database instances that use ASM disks, two new background processes also exist: OSMB and RBAL.

- **OSMB** -- Performs the communication between the database and the ASM instance,
- **RBAL** --- Performs the open and close of the disks in the disk group on behalf of the database instance.

Set up initialization parameter files for ASM and database instances

When installing Oracle ASM in a standalone configuration, Oracle Universal Installer creates a server parameter file for the Oracle ASM instance. The ASM SPFILE is stored in a disk group during installation. For a clustered Oracle ASM environment, OUI creates a single, shared SPFILE for Oracle ASM in a disk group. It's possible to use an SPFILE or a text-based initialization parameter file (PFILE) as the Oracle ASM instance parameter file. Oracle recommends that the Oracle ASM SPFILE is placed in a disk group.

Setting Oracle ASM Initialization Parameters

You can set ASM parameters using the Oracle ASM Configuration Assistant (ASMCA). Some parameters can be set after database creation using Oracle Enterprise Manager or SQL ALTER SYSTEM or ALTER SESSION statements. The Oracle ASM* parameters use suitable defaults for most environments. Any parameters that have names prefixed with Oracle ASM* cannot be used in database instance parameter files. There are several database initialization parameters that are also valid for an Oracle ASM instance and the default values for these are appropriate in most cases. Some of parameters for ASM instances are:

- **ASM_DISKGROUPS** -- Specifies a list of disk groups that an Oracle ASM instance mounts at startup. The default value of the ASM_DISKGROUPS parameter is a NULL string.
- **ASM_DISKSTRING** -- Specifies a comma-delimited list of strings that limits the set of disks that an Oracle ASM instance discovers. The discovery strings can include wildcard characters.
- **ASM_POWER_LIMIT** -- Specifies the default power for disk rebalancing in a disk group. The range of values is 0 to 1024. The default value is 1. A value of 0 disables rebalancing.
- **ASM_PREFERRED_READ_FAILURE_GROUPS** -- Specifies the failure groups that should be preferentially read by the given

instance. Generally used for clustered Oracle ASM instances and its value can be different on different nodes.

- **DB_CACHE_SIZE** -- Determines the size of the buffer cache. Not required when using automatic memory management.
- **DIAGNOSTIC_DEST** -- Specifies the directory where diagnostics for an instance are located. The default value is the $ORACLE_BASE directory.
- **INSTANCE_TYPE** -- Set to ASM for an ASM instance.
- **LARGE_POOL_SIZE** -- Specifies the size of the LARGE_POOL memory area. Not required when using automatic memory management.
- **PROCESSES** -- This parameter affects Oracle ASM, but the default value is usually suitable.
- **SHARED_POOL_SIZE** -- Determines the amount of memory required to manage the instance. The setting for this parameter is also used to determine the amount of space that is allocated for extent storage. Not required when using automatic memory management.

Execute SQL commands with ASM file names

Oracle ASM supports the majority of file types required by the database. The list below shows the most commonly used file types and default template that provides the attributes for file creation. Oracle ASM cannot directly support some administrative file types on disk groups. These include trace files, audit files, alert logs, export files, tar files, and core files.

- **Control files** -- CONTROLFILE
- **Data files** -- DATAFILE
- **Redo log files** -- ONLINELOG
- **Archive log files** -- ARCHIVELOG
- **Temporary files** -- TEMPFILE
- **Data file backup pieces** -- BACKUPSET
- **Archive log backup piece** -- BACKUPSET

- **Persistent initialization parameter file (SPFILE)** -- PARAMETERFILE
- **Flashback logs** -- FLASHBACK
- **Data Pump dumpset** -- DUMPSET

Fully Qualified File Name Form

Whenever a file is created in ASM, Oracle Managed Files automatically generates a fully qualified file name for it. The fully qualified filename represents a complete path name in the Oracle ASM file system. You can use a fully qualified file name for referencing existing Oracle ASM files in Oracle ASM operations, except for disk group creation. A fully qualified file name has the following form:

+diskgroup/dbname/filetype/filetypetag.file.incarnation.

The definitions of the individual elements are:

- **+diskgroup** -- The disk group name preceded by a plus sign. The plus sign (+) is equivalent to the root directory for the Oracle ASM file system.
- **dbname** -- The DB_UNIQUE_NAME of the database to which the file belongs.
- **filetype** -- The Oracle file type and can be one of the file types shown in Table 7–3.
- **filetypetag** -- Type-specific information about the file.
- **file.incarnation** -- The file/incarnation pair, used to ensure uniqueness.

An example of a fully qualified Oracle ASM filename is:

+data/ocpdb/controlfile/Current.221.46544321

The file creation request does not specify the fully qualified filename. It supplies an alias or just a disk group name. Oracle ASM then creates the file in the correct Oracle ASM path based on the file type. ASM then assigns an appropriate fully qualified filename. If an alias is specified in the creation request, ASM creates the alias and points it to the fully qualified filename. ASM file creation requests are either single or multiple file creation requests.

Alias Filenames

Alias filenames can be used for referencing existing files and creating new ASM files. Alias names consist of the disk group name preceded by a plus sign followed by a name string. Alias filenames use a hierarchical directory structure, with the slash (/) or backslash (\) character separating name components. Aliases must include the disk group name. They cannot exist at the root level (+). When a file is created with an alias, both the alias and fully-qualified names are recorded and you can access the file with either name. Alias filenames do not (and cannot) end in a dotted pair of numbers. Examples of alias filenames include:

- +data/ocpdb/control_file_main
- +data/ocpdb/control_file_bkup
- +fra/recover/second.dbf

The example below creates an undo tablespace with a data file that has an alias name, and with attributes that are set by the user-defined template my_undo_template. This example assumes that the ocpdb directory has been created in disk group data.

```
CREATE UNDO TABLESPACE ocpundo
DATAFILE '+data/ocpdb/ocp_undo_ts' SIZE 200M;
```

If an alias is used to create the data file, it is not an Oracle Managed Files (OMF) file. This means that the file will not be automatically deleted when the tablespace is dropped. To drop the file manually after the tablespace has been dropped, use the following SQL statement:

```
ALTER DISKGROUP data DROP FILE '+data/ocpdb/ocp_undo_ts';
```

Use ASMCMD Command-Line Interface

The ASMCMD utility provides a suite of Unix-derived commands in which to access drives and diskgroups accessible to an ASM instance. Three of the most important are cp, lsdsk, and remap.

The cp command can copy files to or from

- ASM diskgroups on a single instance
- ASM diskgroups on local and remote instances
- An ASM diskgroup and the operating system

The lsdsk command lists the disks that are visible to ASM, using the V$ASM_DISK_STAT and V$ASM_DISK views. The V$ASM_DISK_STAT view is used by default. This command can run in connected or non-connected mode. The connected mode is always attempted first. The -i option forces the non-connected mode. Using the connected mode, ASMCMD uses dynamic views to retrieve disk information. Using the non-connected mode, ASMCMD scans disk headers to retrieve disk information.

- -k flag generates detailed information
- -p flag generates disk status
- -s flag generates I/O statistics
- -t flag generates repair information
- -I prefix makes ASM retrieve data from file headers instead of V$ views
- -d flag filters to a specific disk group

The remap command can remap disk sectors. It repairs a range of physical blocks on a disk. The remap command only repairs blocks that have read disk I/O errors. It does not repair blocks that contain corrupted contents, whether or not those blocks can be read.

Start up and shut down ASM instances

Starting an Oracle ASM Instance

An Oracle ASM instance is started much like an Oracle database instance with some minor differences. When starting an Oracle ASM instance, note the following:

You must set the ORACLE_SID environment variable to the Oracle ASM system identifier (SID). The default Oracle ASM SID for a single-instance database is +ASM, and the default SID for Oracle ASM for an Oracle RAC node is +ASMnode_number where node_number is the number of the node. The ORACLE_HOME environment variable must be set to the Grid Infrastructure home where Oracle ASM was installed.

- The initialization parameter file must contain the following entry: INSTANCE_TYPE = ASM This indicates that it is an Oracle ASM instance rather than a database instance.

- When you run the STARTUP command, rather than trying to mount and open a database, this command attempts to mount Oracle ASM disk groups.
- The associated Oracle database instance does not have to be running when you start the associated Oracle ASM instance.

An ASM interprets SQL*Plus STARTUP command parameters differently than a database instance.

- **FORCE** -- Issues a SHUTDOWN ABORT to the Oracle ASM instance before restarting it.
- **MOUNT or OPEN** -- Mounts the disk groups specified in the ASM_DISKGROUPS initialization parameter. This is the default. An OPEN state for an ASM instance doesn't really exist. If supplied, this parameter is simply treated as MOUNT.
- **NOMOUNT** -- Starts up the Oracle ASM instance without mounting any disk groups.
- **RESTRICT** -- Starts up an instance in restricted mode. Only users with both the CREATE SESSION and RESTRICTED SESSION system privileges can connect.

The SYSASM role is similar to the SYSDBA role. It allows users to administer the ASM instance. The SYSASM role was created to provide separation between database administration and disk administration functions (which are normally part of the system administrator's duties).

```
SQLPLUS /NOLOG
SQL> CONNECT SYS AS SYSASM
Enter password: ima_password
Connected to an idle instance.

SQL> STARTUP
ASM instance started
Total System Global Area 71303168 bytes
Fixed Size 1069292 bytes
Variable Size 45068052 bytes
ASM Cache 25165824 bytes
ASM disk groups mounted
```

Shutting Down an Oracle ASM Instance

An ASM is shut down using the SHUTDOWN command in SQL*Plus just as with a database instance. As with startup, you must ensure that the ORACLE_SID environment variable is set to the Oracle ASM SID before connecting to SQL*Plus. Before you shut down an ASM instance, you should shut down all database instances that use it. You should also dismount all file systems mounted on Oracle ASM Dynamic Volume Manager volumes before attempting to shut down the ASM instance.

To shut down an Oracle ASM instance, perform the following steps:

```
SQLPLUS /NOLOG
SQL> CONNECT SYS AS SYSASM
Enter password: ima_password
Connected.
SQL> SHUTDOWN NORMAL
```

The SHUTDOWN modes when used with an Oracle ASM instance are:

- **NORMAL** -- The instance waits for any in-progress SQL to complete before dismounting all of the disk groups and shutting down. The instance also waits for all currently connected users to disconnect from the instance. If any database instances are connected to the ASM instance, then the SHUTDOWN command aborts and returns an error. NORMAL is the default mode.
- **IMMEDIATE or TRANSACTIONAL** -- The instance waits for any in-progress SQL to complete before dismounting all of the disk groups and shutting down the Oracle ASM instance. It does not wait for users currently connected to the instance to disconnect. If any database instances are connected to the Oracle ASM instance, then the SHUTDOWN aborts with an error. ASM instances have no transactions, so TRANSACTIONAL and IMMEDIATE are equivalent.
- **ABORT** -- The instance immediately shuts down without the orderly dismount of disk groups. This requires recovery on the next Oracle ASM startup. Any database instances that are connected to the Oracle ASM instance will also perform a shutdown abort because their storage will no longer be available.

Administer ASM disk groups

An ASM disk group consists of multiple disks and is the fundamental object that Oracle ASM manages. Disk groups contain the information required to manage drive space. The sub-components of disk groups include disks, files, and allocation units. A given file is contained within a single disk group. However, a disk group can contain files from several databases. A single database can use files from multiple disk groups.

Disk Group Attributes

Disk group attributes are parameters that are bound to a disk group rather than an Oracle ASM instance. Some of the more common attributes are below. Refer to the Oracle ASM Administrator's Guide for more details.

- **ACCESS_CONTROL.ENABLED** -- This attribute determines whether Oracle ASM File Access Control is enabled for a disk group. The value can be true or false. The default is false. This attribute can only be set when altering a disk group.
- **ACCESS_CONTROL.UMASK** -- This attribute determines which permissions are masked out on the creation of an Oracle ASM file for the user that owns the file, users in the same user group, and others not in the user group. This attribute applies to all files on a disk group.
- **AU_SIZE** -- A file extent consists of one or more allocation units. An Oracle ASM file consists of one or more file extents. When you create a disk group, you can set the Oracle ASM allocation unit size with the AU_SIZE disk group attribute. The values can be 1, 2, 4, 8, 16, 32, or 64 MB, depending on the specific disk group compatibility level.
- **COMPATIBLE.ASM** -- This attribute controls the format of data structures for ASM metadata in the given disk group. The ASM software version must be equal or greater than this value in order to be able to access the disk group. The COMPATIBLE.ASM attribute must always be greater than or equal to COMPATIBLE.RDBMS for the same disk group. For example, you can set COMPATIBLE.ASM for the disk group to 11.0 and COMPATIBLE.RDBMS for the disk group to 10.1. In this case, the disk group can be managed only by ASM software with a version of 11.0 or higher. However, any database client of version 10.1 or

higher can use the disk group. If you will be increasing both parameters, the COMPATIBLE.ASM value must be increased first.

- **COMPATIBLE.RDBMS** -- This dictates the format of messages that are exchanged between the Automatic Storage Management instance and the database instance. This parameter set the minimum database client release that may access a given disk group. You can set different values of this parameter on diskgroups within the same ASM instance for multiple database clients running at different compatibility settings. Note that the client database level is determined by the value of its own COMPATIBLE initialization parameter. A 10.1 database with a COMPATIBLE parameter value of 9.0.4 is effectively a 9.0.4 database from the standpoint of the ASM instance.
- **CONTENT.TYPE** -- Identifies the disk group type: data, recovery, or system. The type value determines the distance to the nearest neighbor disk in the failure group where Oracle ASM mirrors copies of the data. The default value is 'data' which specifies a distance of 1 to the nearest neighbor disk. A value of 'recovery' specifies a distance of 3 to the nearest neighbor disk and a value of 'system' specifies a distance of 5.
- **DISK_REPAIR_TIME** -- Determines the amount of time that a disk can be unavailable due to a transient failure before to being dropped permanently from the diskgroup. To use this parameter, both the compatible.rdbms and compatible.asm attributes must be set to at least 11.1. You cannot set this attribute when creating a disk group, but you can alter the DISK_REPAIR_TIME attribute in an ALTER DISKGROUP ... SET ATTRIBUTE statement to change the default value. If both compatible.rdbms and compatible.asm are set to at least 11.1, then the default is 3.6 hours. If either parameter is less than 11.1, the disk is dropped immediately if it becomes inaccessible. The time can be specified in units of minutes by using the letter M or hours by using the letter H. If you provide a number with no unit, then the default is hours. The default attribute value can be changed while bringing the disk offline by using an ALTER DISKGROUP ... DISK OFFLINE statement and the DROP AFTER clause. If a disk is taken offline using the current value of DISK_REPAIR_TIME, and the value of this attribute for the diskgroup is subsequently changed with the ALTER DISKGROUP ... SET ATTRIBUTE statement, then the

changed value is used by ASM in determining when to drop the disk.

CREATE DISKGROUP

The CREATE DISKGROUP SQL statement is used to create disk groups. When creating a disk group, you specify the following information:

- A unique name to the disk group.
- The redundancy level of the disk group. For Oracle ASM to mirror files, specify the redundancy level as NORMAL REDUNDANCY (2-way mirroring by default for most file types) or HIGH REDUNDANCY (3-way mirroring for all files). Specify EXTERNAL REDUNDANCY if you do not want mirroring by Oracle ASM.
- The disks that are to be formatted as Oracle ASM disks belonging to the disk group.
- Optionally specify the disks as belonging to specific failure groups.
- Optionally specify the type of failure group.
- Optionally specify disk group attributes, such as software compatibility or allocation unit size.

The SQL statement below creates a disk group named data with normal redundancy. It consists of two failure groups: fg1 or fg2 with three disks in each failure group. The data disk group is typically used to store database data files.

```
CREATE DISKGROUP data NORMAL REDUNDANCY
FAILGROUP fg1 DISK
'/devices/diska1' NAME diska1,
'/devices/diska2' NAME diska2,
'/devices/diska3' NAME diska3
FAILGROUP fg2 DISK
'/devices/diskb1' NAME diskb1,
'/devices/diskb2' NAME diskb2,
'/devices/diskb3' NAME diskb3
ATTRIBUTE 'au_size'='2M',
'compatible.asm' = '11.2',
'compatible.rdbms' = '11.2';
```

ALTER DISKGROUP

The ALTER DISKGROUP SQL statement enables you to alter a disk group configuration. It is possible to add, resize, or drop disks while the database remains online. Multiple operations in a single ALTER DISKGROUP statement are both possible and recommended. Grouping operations in a single ALTER DISKGROUP statement can reduce rebalancing operations. Oracle ASM automatically rebalances a disk group when its configuration changes. The V$ASM_OPERATION view allows you to monitor the status of rebalance operations. The following command adds two more disks to the data diskgroup.

```
ALTER DISKGROUP data ADD DISK
'/devices/diska4' NAME diska4,
'/devices/diska5' NAME diska5;
```

Setup ASM fast mirror resynch

What is fast mirror resynch?

Fast mirror resynch is a new Automated Storage Management feature that allows a disk group to restore redundancy quickly after a transient disk failure. Using 10g ASM with disk group redundancy, if a disk cannot be accessed, it is taken offline and almost immediately dropped. To restore redundancy, the mirror extent copies are resynchronized in the remaining drives of the disk group. This is an extremely costly operation.

Using ASM fast mirror resynch in 11G, if a transient disk failure occurs, the failed drive is automatically taken offline. However, it is not dropped until a predetermined period of time has expired. This time period is set by a new disk group attribute: DISK_REPAIR_TIME. During the time that the drive is offline, ASM tracks modified extents in the disk group. If access to the drive is restored before the drive is dropped, only the modified extents must be resynchronized. Restoring the redundancy is much faster using this process than the 10G model. Fast mirror resynch can only help when the drive failure is transient – a brief power loss, a loose cable, and so forth. If the drive fails such that there is a loss of data, or data corruption, fast mirror resynch cannot help.

DISK_REPAIR_TIME

The default value of the DISK_REPAIR_TIME attribute is 3.6 hours. You may change this by issuing the command:

```
ALTER DISKGROUP dgroupMain SET ATTRIBUTE
'disk_repair_time'='5h';
```

Note that if you provide a number for this attribute with no modifier, the default time increment is hours. You can also take drives offline and set the DISK_REPAIR_TIME if performing maintenance. The following example takes disk D2_001 offline and drops it after five minutes.

```
ALTER DISKGROUP dgroupMain OFFLINE DISK D2_001 DROP AFTER 5m;
```

Alternately, you can offline the disk and leave the drop time equal to the DISK_REPAIR_TIME attribute:

```
ALTER DISKGROUP dgroupMain OFFLINE DISK D2_001;
```

You can determine the current setting of the DISK_REPAIR_TIME attribute for the diskgroups in your ASM instance from the V$ASM_ATTRIBUTE view:

```
SELECT group_number, name, value
FROM   v$asm_attribute
WHERE  name='disk_repair_time';

GROUP_NUMBER NAME                  VALUE
------------ --------------------- ------------
           1 disk_repair_time      3.6h
           2 disk_repair_time      3.6h
```

Understand scalability and performance enhancements

ASM Preferred Mirror Read

In Oracle 10g, if there were multiple failure groups, ASM would always reads the primary copy of the mirrored extent set. In a non-RAC database, or one where all nodes and failure groups are located at the same site, this behavior is not an issue. However, for an Oracle installation where there is a Real Application Cluster with failure groups and instances spread among two or more locations, it could cause significant network traffic. With Oracle 11g there is a new capability that allows each node to define a preferred failure group to read from. This would allow nodes in extended clusters to access drives from their local failure groups in preference to remote drives. This allows for faster access and lower impact to network bandwidth. The new ASM_PREFERRED_READ_FAILURE_GROUPS parameter is used to set the preferred failure groups for each node.

```
ALTER SYSTEM SET asm_preferred_read_failure_groups =
      'DGROUPA.DGROUPA_000', 'DGROUPB.DGROUPB_000';
```

Variable ASM Allocation Units

ASM files are stored in a disk group as a group of extents. In Oracle 10g a single extent mapped to a single allocation unit (AU) of a set size -- 1MB. The larger an ASM file gets, the more extents it has, and the more extent pointers are required in the SGA to describe the file. Oracle 11G reduces the number of extents required by ASM files in two ways. First, when you create a disk group in 11G, you can set the ASM Allocation Unit size to be between 1 MB and 64 MB in powers of two, such as, 1, 2, 4, 8, 16, 32, or 64. Larger AU sizes typically provide performance advantages for data warehouse applications that use large sequential reads. Second, in Oracle 11g the concept of variable size extents means that an extent can consist of one or more allocation units. The first 20,000 extents for a disk group will match the allocation unit size (1*AU). The next 20,000 extents will be made up of 8 allocation units (8*AU). Beyond that point, the extent size becomes 64 allocation units (64*AU). The combination of the two new features significantly reduces memory requirements for very large databases.

SQL Performance Analyzer

Using SQL Performance Analyzer

Changes to your database, whether major (such as an upgrade of the Oracle version), or minor (like adding an index) are likely to cause changes to SQL execution plans. While the hope is that these will cause a performance improvement, in some cases, the system changes may cause performance degradation. SQL Performance Analyzer is a tool that can accurately forecast the potential impact of system changes on SQL performance. By doing so, it allows you to tune the system beforehand in cases where SQL statements regress. If the performance of SQL statements will improve, verifying that ahead of time is also valuable information. SQL Performance Analyzer automates the process of assessing the impact of a change on the SQL workload. It identifies performance divergence for each SQL statement and provides a report that shows the net impact of the change on the workload performance. For regressed SQL statements, it provides execution plan details along with tuning recommendations.

SQL Performance Analyzer can be run on a production database or a test database that closely resembles it. Performing the test on the production system will impact its throughput because SQL Performance Analyzer must execute the SQL statements being tested. Changes made to the system for the test may also affect the database users. Testing major changes (such as a database upgrade) using a production system is not recommended. For changes of that magnitude, you should run SQL Performance Analyzer on a separate test system so that you don't impact the production system.

For the test, be sure that you understand the difference between the SQL Performance Analyzer and the SQL Tuning Advisor. The SQL Performance Analyzer is designed to help determine the impact of system changes to SQL performance. The SQL Tuning Advisor is designed to help tune SQL in the system as it currently exists.

Sources of SQL statements

Before running the SQL Performance Analyzer, you must capture the SQL statements from the production system that you intend to analyze.

Capturing a SQL workload has a negligible performance impact on a production system. Capturing a workload that contains large number SQL statements will better represent the production system database. This will assist SQL Performance Analyzer in accurately forecasting the potential impact of system changes. Ideally, you should capture all SQL statements that are either called by the application or are running on the production database. Captured SQL statements can be stored in a SQL tuning set and used as an input for SQL Performance Analyzer. A SQL tuning set is a database object that includes one or more SQL statements, along with their execution statistics and execution context. SQL statements can be loaded into a SQL tuning set from many different sources. It's possible to use the cursor cache, Automatic Workload Repository (AWR), or existing SQL tuning sets.

The following views allow you to monitor SQL Performance Analyzer and view its analysis results:

- **DBA_ADVISOR_TASKS** -- displays descriptive information about the SQL Performance Analyzer task that was created.
- **DBA_ADVISOR_EXECUTIONS** -- displays information about task executions.
- **DBA_ADVISOR_FINDINGS** -- displays the SQL Performance Analyzer findings.
- **DBA_ADVISOR_SQLPLANS** -- displays a list of all execution plans.
- **DBA_ADVISOR_SQLSTATS** -- displays a list of all SQL compilations and execution statistics.
- **V$ADVISOR_PROGRESS** -- displays the operation progress of SQL Performance Analyzer.

Steps in analyzing performance changes

1. Capture the SQL workload that you intend to analyze and store it in a SQL tuning set.
2. If you plan to use a test system separate from your production system, then set up the test system to match the production environment as closely as possible and transport the SQL tuning set to the test system.
3. On the test system, create a SQL Performance Analyzer task.

4. Build the pre-change SQL trial by executing the SQL statements stored in the SQL tuning set.
5. Perform the system change.
6. Build the post-change SQL trial by re-executing the SQL statements in the SQL tuning set on the post-change test system.
7. Compare and analyze the pre-change and post-change versions of performance data, and generate a report to identify the SQL statements that have improved, remained unchanged or regressed after the system change.
8. Tune any regressed SQL statements that are identified.

Processes

Several procedures in the DBMS_SQLTUNE package allow you to create, import and export SQL tuning Sets:

- **CREATE_SQLSET** -- creates a SQL tuning set object in the database.
- **LOAD_SQLSET** -- This procedure populates the SQL tuning set with a set of selected SQL. You can call the procedure multiple times to add new SQL statements or replace attributes of existing statements.
- **CREATE_SGTAB_SQLSET** -- This procedure creates a staging table through which SQL Tuning Sets are imported and exported.
- **PACK_STGTAB_SQLSET** -- This procedure copies one or more SQL tuning sets from their location in the SYS schema to a staging table created by the CREATE_STGTAB_SQLSET Procedure.
- **UNPACK_STGTAB_SQLSET** -- This procedure copies one or more SQL tuning sets from their location in the staging table into the SQL tuning sets schema, making them proper SQL tuning sets.

The DBMS_SQLPA package contains procedures and functions specific to the SQL Performance Analyzer. These are used to create and execute analyses and report on their findings:

- **CREATE_ANALYSIS_TASK** -- You can use different forms of this function to create analysis tasks for: a single SQL statement from various sources (the SQL text, the AWR, or the cursor cache) or for a SQL tuning set.
- **EXECUTE_ANALYSIS_TASK** -- This function and procedure executes a previously created analysis task, the function version returning the new execution name.
- **REPORT_ANALYSIS_TASK** -- This procedure displays the results of an analysis task.

SQL Plan Management

SQL Plan Baseline Architecture

Oracle's SQL plan management is intended to prevent performance regressions resulting from sudden changes to the execution plan of a SQL statement. It does so by providing components for capturing, selecting, and evolving SQL plan information. SQL Plan execution can be affected by various changes, such as changes to the optimizer version, statistics, schema, system settings or the application of SQL profiles. Some events, such as dropping an index, can cause irreversible changes to an execution plan. Any number of events can cause regressions in SQL performance, and fixing them can be difficult and time consuming. The SQL Tuning Advisor generates SQL profiles designed to help the optimizer produce well-tuned plans. However, this is a reactive mechanism and can only resolve performance issues after they have occurred and are identified. SQL plan management is a preventative mechanism that records and evaluates the execution plans of SQL statements over time. It builds SQL plan baselines composed of execution plans known to be efficient. The baselines are used to preserve performance of SQL statements, regardless of changes that occur in the system.

SYSAUX Tablespace

The SQL management base (SMB) is a part of the data dictionary and resides in the SYSAUX tablespace. SMB stores statement logs, plan histories, SQL plan baselines, and SQL profiles. The SMB is configured with automatic space management enabled which enables weekly purging of unused plans and logs. Because the SMB is stored entirely within the SYSAUX tablespace, SQL plan management and SQL tuning features will not be used if SYSAUX is not available. The SQL Management base will use a set percentage of the SYSAUX tablespace. By default, the SMB will use no more than 10% of the SYSAUX tablespace. You can set this range between 1% and 50%. A weekly background process measures the total space occupied by the SMB, and will generate a warning in the alert log when the defined limit is exceeded. The alerts continue to be generated weekly until the SMB space limit is increased, the size of the SYSAUX tablespace is increased, or the disk space used by the SMB is decreased.

You can change the percentage limit, with the CONFIGURE procedure of the DBMS_SPM package:

```
DBMS_SPM.CONFIGURE('space_budget_percent',30);
```

Weekly, a scheduled purging task manages the disk space used by SQL plan management. The task runs as an automated task in the maintenance window. It will purge any plan that has not been used for more than 53 weeks. Unused plans are identified by the LAST_EXECUTED timestamp stored in the SMB for that plan. The unused plan retention period can range between 5 weeks and 523 weeks. You can use the DBMS_SPM.CONFIGURE procedure to configure the retention period:

```
DBMS_SPM.CONFIGURE('plan_retention_weeks',105);
```

The current configuration settings for the SQL management base can be viewed using the DBA_SQL_MANAGEMENT_CONFIG view:

```
SELECT parameter_name, parameter_value
FROM   dba_sql_management_config;

PARAMETER_NAME           PARAMETER_VALUE
------------------------ ---------------
SPACE_BUDGET_PERCENT                  30
PLAN_RETENTION_WEEKS                 105
```

Set up SQL Plan Baseline

Automatic Plan Capture

Oracle will automatically create and maintain the plan history for SQL statements using information provided by the optimizer when automatic plan capture is enabled. The plan history will include information required by the optimizer to reproduce an execution plan. This includes the SQL text, outline, bind variables, and compilation environment. The first time a plan is generated for a given SQL statement, that plan is marked as accepted for use by the optimizer. That initial plan represents both the plan history and the SQL plan baseline. Any subsequent plans for that SQL statement will be included in the plan history. Any of these later plans that are verified not to cause performance regressions will be added to the SQL plan baseline during the SQL plan baseline evolution phase. The initialization parameter OPTIMIZER_CAPTURE_SQL_PLAN_BASELINES must be set to TRUE to enable automatic plan capture. By default, this parameter is set to FALSE.

Loading Plans Manually

It's also possible to manually create SQL plan baselines. You do this by loading existing plans for a set of SQL statements as SQL plan baselines. The manually loaded plans are not verified for performance, but are added as accepted plans immediately. You can use manual plan loading by itself, or in addition to automatic plan capture. You can load plans from SQL Tuning Sets and AWR Snapshots, or the Cursor Cache.

- **DBMS_SPM.LOAD_PLANS_FROM_SQLSET** -- Allows you to load plans from a SQL Tuning Set. To load plans from Automatic Workload Repository (AWR), you must first load the plans stored in AWR snapshots into a SQL Tuning Set using the CREATE_SQLSET and LOAD_SQLSET procedures.
- **DBMS_SPM.LOAD_PLANS_FROM_CURSOR_CACHE** -- Allows you to load plans from the cursor cache.

Using SQL Plan Baseline

Selecting SQL Plan Baselines

When selecting from stored baseline plans for a given SQL statement, the Oracle database detects plan changes based on the stored plan history. It will select a plan to avoid potential performance regression for a given statement. Whenever a SQL statement is compiled, the optimizer initially uses a cost-based search to build a best-cost plan. It will then try to locate a match in the SQL plan baseline. If one is found, the optimizer will make use of the matching plan. If no match is found, it evaluates the cost of each accepted plan in the SQL plan baseline and uses the plan with the lowest cost. If the best-cost plan generated by the optimizer does not match any plans in the plan history for the SQL statement, it is added as a non-accepted plan to the plan history. The new plan will not be used until it is verified to not cause a performance regression. If a change in the system (such as a dropped index) causes all accepted plans to become non-reproducible, the optimizer will select the best-cost plan without regard to its acceptance status. To enable the use of SQL plan baselines, you must set the OPTIMIZER_USE_SQL_PLAN_BASELINES initialization parameter to TRUE (default).

Evolving SQL Plan Baselines

In order for new plans in the SQL plan history to be used, they must be accepted. Acceptance of SQL Plans occurs during the SQL Plan baseline evolution phase. During this phase, the database evaluates the performance of new plans and integrates the best plans into SQL plan baselines. When a non-accepted plan is verified to not cause a performance regression, it is changed to an accepted plan and integrated into the SQL plan baseline. A successful verification of a non-accepted plan consists of comparing it to an accepted plan in the SQL plan baseline and ensuring the new plan delivers better performance. Existing SQL plan baselines can be evolved by manually loading plans either from the cursor cache or from a SQL tuning set. Manually loaded plans are automatically added as accepted plans. The PL/SQL function DBMS_SPM.EVOLVE_SQL_PLAN_BASELINE attempts to evolve new plans added by the optimizer to the SQL plan history. If EVOLVE_SQL_PLAN_BASELINE can verify that the new plan performs better than an accepted plan chosen from the corresponding SQL plan baseline, it is added as an accepted plan.

Fixed Plans

A SQL plan baseline is defined as 'fixed' if it contains at least one enabled plan that has the FIXED attribute set to YES. Fixed SQL plan baselines are used to limit the set of possible plans (usually one plan) for a SQL statement. They can also be used to migrate an existing stored outline by loading the "outlined" plan as a fixed plan. When a fixed SQL plan baseline also contains non-fixed plans, the optimizer gives preference to fixed plans over non-fixed ones. The optimizer will pick the fixed plan with the least cost over a non-fixed plan with an even lower cost. Only if none of the fixed plans is reproducible, will the optimizer will pick a non-fixed plan. The optimizer will not automatically add new plans to a fixed SQL plan baseline. Because new plans are not automatically added, DBMS_SPM.EVOLVE_SQL_PLAN_BASELINE does not evolve a fixed SQL plan baseline. A fixed SQL plan baseline can only be evolved by manually loading new plans into it. If the SQL Tuning Advisor creates a profile for a SQL statement with a fixed SQL plan baseline, by default that profile won't be used. The tuned plan is added to the fixed SQL plan baseline as a non-fixed plan. Since non-fixed plans aren't used except by necessity when a SQL Plan is fixed, in order for the tuned plan to be utilized, you must manually alter the tuned plan to a fixed plan by setting its FIXED attribute to YES.

Displaying SQL Plan Baselines

You can view the plans stored in the SQL plan baseline for a given statement by using the DISPLAY_SQL_PLAN_BASELINE function of the DBMS_XPLAN package. This function displays one or more execution plans for the specified SQL statement, specified by the sql_handle. You can display a single plan by supplying a plan name. The function uses plan information stored in the SQL management base to explain and display the plans.

```
SELECT *
FROM   table(dbms_xplan.display_sql_plan_baseline(
                 sql_handle   => 'SYS_SQL_109c10fabeeec639',
                 format       => 'basic')
            );
```

Database Replay

Overview of Workload Capture and Replay

When to use Database Replay

Before making significant hardware or software upgrades to a production Oracle database, typically extensive testing is performed to verify the changes will not adversely affect the system. However, making such testing close enough to reality to provide a valid test is very difficult. Often problems are encountered after the upgrade that were not located during the testing period. There are various third-party tools on the market to provide load testing for Oracle, simulating the workload from multiple users. However, the workloads generated are not as complex and interactive as that generated by a real production system. Oracle 11G's new Database Replay feature enables system administrators to perform real-world testing by capturing the production database workload and replaying it on another database. In addition, it provides analysis and reporting of potential problems and recommend ways to resolve these problems.

What is captured by Database Replay

Oracle Database Replay captures all external database calls made to the system during the workload capture period. The capture includes all relevant information about the client request, such as SQL text, bind values, and transaction information. Background activities of the database and scheduler jobs are not captured. In addition, the following types of client requests are not captured in a workload:

- Direct path load of data from external files using utilities such as SQL*Loader
- Shared server requests (Oracle MTS)
- Oracle Streams
- Advanced replication streams
- Non-PL/SQL based Advanced Queuing (AQ)
- Flashback queries
- Oracle Call Interface (OCI) based object navigations
- Non SQL-based object access
- Distributed transactions

Using Workload capture and replay

It is a best practice to restart the database before capturing the production workload. This ensures that ongoing and dependent transactions are allowed to be completed or rolled back before the capture begins. If the database is not restarted before the capture, transactions that are in progress or have yet to be committed will be only partially captured in the workload.

Define Workload Filters

By default, all activities from all user sessions are recorded during workload capture. Workload filters can be used to include or exclude specific user sessions during the workload capture. You can use either inclusion filters or exclusion filters in a workload capture, but not both simultaneously. Inclusion filters specify user sessions that will be captured in the workload. Exclusion filters enable you to specify user sessions that will not be captured in the workload. To add filters to a workload capture, you use the DBMS_WORKLOAD_CAPTURE.ADD_FILTER procedure. To remove an existing filter, you use the DBMS_WORKLOAD_CAPTURE.DELETE_FILTER procedure.

Setting Up the Capture Directory

Before starting the workload capture, you must decide on the directory where the captured workload will be stored. Before starting the capture, verify that the directory is empty and has enough space for the workload. If the directory runs out of disk space during a workload capture, the capture will stop.

Starting a Workload Capture

You should have a well-defined starting point for the workload so that the database being used to replay the workload can be restored to the same point before starting the captured workload. It is best not to have any active user sessions when starting a workload capture. Active sessions may have ongoing transactions which will not be replayed completely. Consider restarting the database in RESTRICTED mode prior to starting the workload capture. When the workload capture begins, the database will automatically switch to UNRESTRICTED mode and normal operations can continue while the workload is being captured. You begin a workload capture using the procedure DBMS_WORKLOAD_CAPTURE.START_CAPTURE.

Stopping a Workload Capture

To stop a workload capture in progress, you use the FINISH_CAPTURE procedure of the DBMS_WORKLOAD_CAPTURE package.

Exporting AWR Data for Workload Capture

You can export AWR data from the production machine in order to enable detailed analysis of the workload on both systems. This data is required if you plan to run the AWR Compare Period report on a pair of workload captures or replays. To export AWR data, you use the DBMS_WORKLOAD_CAPTURE.EXPORT_AWR procedure.

Workload Capture Views

The following views allow you to monitor a workload capture. You can also use Oracle Enterprise Manager to monitor a workload capture:

- **DBA_WORKLOAD_CAPTURES** -- Lists all the workload captures that have been created in the current database.
- **DBA_WORKLOAD_FILTERS** -- Lists all workload filters used for workload captures defined in the current database.

Preparing the Replay

After the workload has been captured, it's necessary to preprocess the capture files prior to using them in a replay. Preprocessing converts the captured data into replay files and creates the required metadata needed to replay the workload. After preprocessing the captured workload, it can be replayed multiple times on any replay system running the same version of Oracle. As a general rule, it's recommended to move the capture files to another system for preprocessing. While the capture itself has a minimal overhead, workload preprocessing can be time consuming and resource intensive. It is better that this step be performed on the test system where the workload will be replayed rather than on the production database. Capture files are processed using the PROCESS_CAPTURE procedure of the DBMS_WORKLOAD_REPLAY package.

Replaying the Workload

After you have preprocessed a captured workload, it can be replayed on the test system. In the workload replay, Oracle will perform the actions recorded during the workload capture. It will re-create all captured external client requests with the same timing, concurrency, and transaction dependencies that occurred on the production system. Database Replay uses a program called the replay client to re-create the external client requests. You may need to use multiple replay clients depending on the scope of the captured workload. The replay client has an imbedded calibration tool to help determine the number of replay clients required for a given workload. The entire workload from the production database is replayed. This includes DML and SQL queries, so the data in the replay system must be as logically similar to the data in the capture system as possible. Ensuring the systems are as identical as possible will minimize data divergence and enable a more reliable analysis of the replay. Replaying a database workload requires the following steps:

Setting Up the Replay Directory

The captured workload must have been preprocessed and copied to the replay system. An Oracle directory object for the directory to which the preprocessed workload has been copied must exist in the replay system.

Resolving References to External Systems

A captured workload may contain references to external systems, such as database links or external tables. These should be reconfigured to avoid impacting production systems during replay. External references that need to be resolved before replaying a workload include: Database links, external tables, directory objects, URLs, and e-mail addresses. If these external connections are not changed before starting the replay, you could end up changing data in production systems, sending emails to users, and other undesirable actions.

Remapping Connections

Connection strings used to connect to the production system are captured in the workload. You must remap these connection strings to the replay system for the replay to succeed. The clients can then connect to the replay system using the remapped connections. For Oracle Real Application Cluster databases, you can map all connection strings to a load balancing connection string.

Specifying Replay Options

There are several options that determine the behavior of the database replay.

- **synchronization** -- determines whether the COMMIT order will be preserved during replay. By default, synchronization is enabled. All transactions will be executed only after all dependent transactions have been committed. If you disable this option, the replay will likely have significant data divergence. This may be not be a problem if the workload consists primarily of independent transactions. Not preserving the commit order can also lead to a faster replay, if 'stress testing' of the replay system is desirable.
- **connect_time_scale** -- enables you to scale the elapsed time between the time when the sessions connected to the database during the workload capture began and when each session connects during the replay. This option allows you to manipulate the session connect time during replay with a given percentage value. By default, the value is 100, which will attempt to connect all sessions as captured. Setting this parameter to 0 will attempt to connect all sessions immediately.
- **think_time_scale** -- allows you to scale user think time during replay. User think time is the elapsed time while the replayed user waits between issuing calls within a single session. A value of 100 means that time between calls will be the same as they were during the capture. A value of zero will eliminate all wait time between calls.
- **think_time_auto_correct** -- If user calls are being executed slower during replay than during capture, you can make the database replay attempt to catch up by setting this parameter to TRUE. When set to true, it will make the replay client shorten the think time between calls, so that the overall elapsed time of the replay will more closely match the captured elapsed time.

Setting Up Replay Clients

The replay client is a multithreaded program where each thread submits a workload from a captured session. It is an executable file named wrc located in the $ORACLE_HOME/bin directory. The replay user that wrc logs in as needs the DBA role and cannot be SYS. The wrc executable uses the following syntax:

```
wrc [user/pword[@server]] MODE=[value] [keyword=[value]]
```

The mode parameter specifies the action to be taken when the wrc executable is run. Possible values include replay (the default), calibrate, and list_hosts. The parameter keyword specifies the options to use for the execution and is dependent on the mode selected. To display the possible keywords and their corresponding values, run the wrc executable without any arguments. The modes that you can select when running the wrc executable and their corresponding keywords are:

- **replay (the default)** -- runs a captured workload. In replay mode, the wrc executable accepts the following keywords:
  - ✓ **userid and password** -- specify the user ID and password of a replay user for the replay client. If unspecified, the user ID defaults to the SYSTEM user.
  - ✓ **server** -- specifies the connection string that is used to connect to the replay system. If unspecified, the value defaults to an empty string.
  - ✓ **replaydir** -- specifies the directory that contains the preprocessed workload capture you want to replay. If unspecified, it defaults to the current directory.
  - ✓ **debug** -- specifies whether debug data will be created.
  - ✓ **workdir** -- specifies the directory where the client logs will be written. This parameter is only used in conjunction with the debug parameter.
  - ✓ **connection_override** -- specifies whether to override the connection mappings stored in the DBA_WORKLOAD_CONNECTION_MAP view.
- **calibrate** -- causes wrc to return an estimate of the number of replay clients and hosts that are required to replay a particular workload. In calibration mode, wrc accepts the following keywords:
  - ✓ **replaydir** -- specifies the directory that contains the preprocessed workload capture. It defaults to the current directory.
  - ✓ **process_per_cpu** -- specifies the maximum number of client processes that can run per CPU. The default value is 4.

  - ✓ **threads_per_process** -- specifies the maximum number of threads that can run within a client process. The default value is 50.
- list_hosts -- Displays the hosts that participated in a workload capture and workload replay. In list_hosts mode, the wrc executable accepts only one keyword:
  - ✓ replaydir -- specifies the directory that contains the preprocessed workload capture you want to replay. If unspecified, it defaults to the current directory

Analysis and Reporting

Once the workload replay has completed, in-depth reporting is available so that you can perform detailed analysis of both the workload capture and the replay operation. The summary report provides basic information such as errors encountered during replay and data divergence in rows returned by DML or SQL queries. A comparison of several statistics between the source and replay servers is also provided. You can use Automatic Workload Repository reports for advanced analysis of the workload processing between the two servers.

Miscellaneous New Features

Describe and use the enhanced online table redefinition

Oracle Database provides a mechanism called online table redefinition to make table structure modifications without significantly affecting its availability. When a table is redefined online, it is accessible to both queries and DML during much of the redefinition process. Only during a very small window is the table is locked in the exclusive mode. The window is independent of the size of the table and complexity of the redefinition. Other than the period during which the table must be locked, the redefinition is transparent to users. In Oracle 11G, there have been enhancements to the online table redefinition process that have reduced the impact even further.

- In previous releases, a table could not be redefined if it had a log or materialized views defined. With Oracle 11G, this restriction has been lifted.
- Oracle 11G has eliminated the need for DML-blocking locks when creating or rebuilding an online index. Online index creation and rebuild prior to 11G required a DML-blocking lock at the beginning and end of the rebuild for a short period of time. This lock is no longer required, making these online index operations fully transparent.
- If a table redefinition does not logically affect PL/SQL packages that reference the table, recompilation is not needed. This reduces the time and effort to manually recompile dependent PL/SQL objects after an online table redefinition. This feature extends to views, synonyms, and other table dependent objects (with the exception of triggers) that are not logically affected by the redefinition.

Use fine-grained auditing for DML statements

Fine-grained auditing (FGA) allows for the creation of policies that define specific conditions that trigger an audit record. It provides the ability to perform content-based auditing of queries, and DML operations. Policies are based on user-defined SQL predicates on table objects as conditions for selective auditing. If policy conditions are met for a row on a give SQL operation, an audit record is created. To create a fine-grained audit policy, you must have EXECUTE privileges on the DBMS_FGA PL/SQL package. Fine-grained auditing policies can be triggered by many things, including:

- Accessing a table between a given set of hours or a given set of days.
- Access from an IP address outside the corporate network
- Selecting or updating a specific table column

Fine-grained auditing creates a more meaningful audit trail than standard auditing. It has the following advantages over standard auditing:

- Performs a Boolean condition check. An audit record is only created if the Boolean condition you specify is met.
- It can capture the SQL that triggered the audit. You can capture both the SQL statement that caused the audit, and any associated bind variables. The SQL capture feature is available if you create the fine grained audit policy with the audit_trail parameter of the DBMS_FGA.ADD_POLICY PL/SQL procedure to DB+EXTENDED or XML+EXTENDED.
- You can audit specific relevant columns that may hold sensitive information, such as salaries or Social Security numbers.
- It provides an event handler feature that can perform tasks such as sending an e-mail alert to a security administrator.
- Initialization parameters are not required to enable fine-grained auditing. The DBMS_FGA PL/SQL package is used to add and remove fine-grained auditing policies as necessary.

The audit trail format for fine-grained auditing is specified using the audit_trail parameter of the DBMS_FGA.ADD_POLICY policy. This has no relation to the AUDIT_TRAIL initialization parameter. Setting this parameter to XML or XML+EXTENDED writes the records to the operating system files in XML format. To write audit records to the SYS.FGA_LOG$ table, the audit_trail parameter is set to DB or DB+EXTENDED.

The DBMS_FGA package enables you to add all combinations of SELECT, INSERT, UPDATE, and DELETE statements to a single policy. The audit policy is bound to the table for which you created it. If any rows returned from a query match the audit condition, then the Database creates an audit entry. To create a fine-grained audit policy, use the DBMS_FGA.ADD_POLICY procedure. You cannot modify a fine-grained audit policy after you have created it. If you need to modify the policy, drop it and then recreate it. Be aware that if a table column has a fine-grained audit policy, you cannot encrypt or decrypt this column.

The syntax for the ADD_POLICY procedure is:

```
DBMS_FGA.ADD_POLICY(
  object_schema      VARCHAR2,
  object_name        VARCHAR2,
  policy_name        VARCHAR2,
  audit_condition    VARCHAR2,
  audit_column       VARCHAR2,
  handler_schema     VARCHAR2,
  handler_module     VARCHAR2,
  enable             BOOLEAN,
  statement_types    VARCHAR2,
  audit_trail        BINARY_INTEGER IN DEFAULT,
  audit_column_opts  BINARY_INTEGER IN DEFAULT);
```

The parameter specifications are:

- **object_schema**-- The schema of the object to be audited (or NULL for the current schema)
- **object_name** -- The name of the object to be audited.
- **policy_name** -- The name of the policy to be created. Ensure that this name is unique.
- **audit_condition** -- Boolean condition in a row. NULL is allowed and acts as TRUE. When NULL, any action on a table with that policy creates an audit record.
- **audit_column** -- Columns to audit, including hidden columns. If set to NULL, all columns are audited.
- **handler_schema** -- If an alert is used to trigger a response when the policy is violated, specifies the name of the schema that contains the event handler. The default, NULL, uses the current schema.
- **handler_module** -- The event handler invoked on the first row that matches the audit condition when the query is processed. If the procedure fails with an exception, then the user SQL statement fails as well.

- **enable** -- Enables or disables the policy using true or false. The default is TRUE.
- **statement_types** -- The SQL statements to be audited: INSERT, UPDATE, DELETE, or SELECT only.
- **audit_trail** -- The destination (DB or XML) of fine-grained audit records. Also specifies whether to populate LSQLTEXT and LSQLBIND in FGA_LOG$.

Tables and views related to Fine-grained Auditing

- **SYS.FGA_LOG$** -- Fine-grained auditing records are stored in this table.
- **DBA_FGA_AUDIT_TRAIL** -- This view contains records have been generated for the audit policies that are in effect
- **DBA_COMMON_AUDIT_TRAIL** -- This view combines both standard and fine-grained audit log records.
- **V$XML_AUDIT_TRAIL** -- This view contains fine-grained audit records that were written in XML formatted files.

Use Enhanced DDL - Apply the improved table lock mechanism, Create invisible indexes

Waits for DDL operations

In order to work properly, data definition language (DDL) commands require exclusive locks on internal structures. At the time a DDL command is issued, there might be DML operations against the target object. If so, an exclusive lock won't be immediately available, and will cause the DDL statement to fail. This happens even though the DDL could have possibly succeeded if the command had been issued a second later. In Oracle 11G, this can be resolved by setting the WAIT option in the DDL_LOCK_TIMEOUT initialization parameter. The wait time is specified instance-wide in the initialization parameter file, but can be modified at the session level. The WAIT option provides more flexibility to define grace periods for DDL commands to succeed. To specify a DDL lock timeout, the DDL_LOCK_TIMEOUT parameter must be set to an integer value that sets the number of seconds a DDL statement will wait for an exclusive lock. The permissible range of values for DDL_LOCK_TIMEOUT is 0 to 100,000. The default is 0. You can set DDL_LOCK_TIMEOUT at the system level using an ALTER SYSTEM statement, or at the session level with an ALTER SESSION statement.

Invisible Indexes

Beginning with Oracle Database 11g, it's possible to create invisible indexes or make an existing index invisible. Invisible indexes are ignored by the optimizer unless the OPTIMIZER_USE_INVISIBLE_INDEXES initialization parameter is set to TRUE at the session or system level. An invisible index is maintained during DML statements, unlike an unusable index. It is possible to make a partitioned index invisible, but it is not possible to make an individual index partition invisible while leaving the other partitions visible. Invisible indexes are useful in the following cases:

- Test the removal of an index before dropping it.
- Using indexes for certain operations or modules of an application without affecting the overall application.

To create an invisible index, you make use of the INVISIBLE keyword of the CREATE INDEX statement. The following statement creates an invisible index named emp_ename for the ename column of the emp table:

```
CREATE INDEX emp_ename ON emp(ename)
  TABLESPACE users
  STORAGE (INITIAL 200K
           NEXT 200k)
  INVISIBLE;
```

To make an index invisible, use the INVISIBLE keyword of the ALTER INDEX CLAUSE:

```
ALTER INDEX index_name INVISIBLE;
```

To make an invisible index visible again, use the VISIBLE keyword of the ALTER INDEX clause:

```
ALTER INDEX index VISIBLE;
```

To determine whether an index is visible or invisible, you can query the dictionary views USER_INDEXES, ALL_INDEXES, or DBA_INDEXES.

For example, to determine if the index EMP_ENAME is invisible, issue the following query:

```
SELECT index_name, visibility
FROM   USER_INDEXES
WHERE  index_name = 'EMP_ENAME';

INDEX_NAME VISIBILITY
---------- ----------
EMP_ENAME  INVISIBLE
```

Use Query Result Cache and PL/SQL Result Cache

In Oracle 11G, a separate shared memory pool called the Result Cache Memory is now available. The result cache stores the results of SQL queries and PL/SQL functions. When these queries and functions are executed repeatedly, the results are retrieved directly from the cache, resulting in a faster response time. The cached results are automatically invalidated when data in the dependent database objects is modified. The Result Cache Memory pool consists of the SQL Query Result Cache, which stores the results of SQL queries, and the PL/SQL Function Result Cache, which stores the values returned by PL/SQL functions. Query results that are bigger than the available space in the result cache will not be cached.

The use of the SQL query result cache can be controlled by setting the RESULT_CACHE_MODE initialization parameter. The possible values are MANUAL and FORCE. When set to MANUAL, you must use the result_cache hint in a SQL Query for its results to be cached.

```
SELECT /*+ result_cache */ deptno, AVG(sal)
FROM   emp
GROUP BY deptno;
```

If the result is not already available in the cache, then the query will be executed and the result stored in the cache. Subsequent executions of the statement (including the result cache hint) will use results from the cache. When the RESULT_CACHE_MODE parameter is set to FORCE, all SQL results use the cache by default. Using the no_result_cache hint in SQL statements will bypass the cache when using the FORCE mode.

```
SELECT /*+ no_result_cache */ deptno, AVG(sal)
FROM   emp
GROUP BY deptno;
```

You cannot cache results when you use the following database objects or functions in your SQL query:

- Dictionary and temporary tables
- Sequence CURRVAL and NEXTVAL pseudo columns
- SQL functions current_date, current_timestamp, local_timestamp, sys_guid, sysdate, and sys_timestamp
- Non-deterministic PL/SQL functions

Parameterized cache results can be reused if the query is equivalent and the parameter values are the same. Cached results are parameterized with the parameter values if any of the following constructs are used in the query:

- Bind variables.
- The following SQL functions: dbtimezone, uid, user, and sessiontimezone.
- NLS parameters.

Result Cache Parameters

- **RESULT_CACHE_MAX_SIZE** -- allows you to change the memory allocated to the result cache. The result cache is disabled if you set the value to 0 during database startup.
- **RESULT_CACHE_MAX_RESULT** -- specifies the maximum percentage of result cache memory that can be used by any single

result. The default value is 5%, but you can specify any percent value between 1 and 100.

- **RESULT_CACHE_REMOTE_EXPIRATION** -- specifies the time (in minutes) for which a result that accesses remote database objects remains valid. When set to 0 (the default), the SQL query result cache is disabled for queries that access remote tables. Note that when you use a non-zero value, a DML on the remote database will not invalidate the result cache.

DBMS_RESULT_CACHE

The DBMS_RESULT_CACHE package allows the DBA to administer the portion of the shared pool used by the SQL and PL/SQL function result caches. Both these caches use the same infrastructure so DBMS_RESULT_CACHE operations affect both caches simultaneously. The DBMS_RESULT_CACHE package can be used to perform various operations such as bypassing the cache, retrieving statistics on the cache memory usage, and flushing the cache.

- **DBMS_RESULT_CACHE.BYPASS** -- sets the bypass mode for the Result Cache. When bypass mode is turned on, cached results are no longer used and no new results are saved. When bypass mode is turned off, the cache resumes normal operation.
- **DBMS_RESULT_CACHE.FLUSH** -- attempts to remove all the objects from the Result Cache, and depending on the arguments retains or releases the memory and retains or clears the statistics. Prior to flushing the cache, you should set BYPASS to ON.
- **DBMS_RESULT_CACHE.INVALIDATE** -- invalidates all the result-set objects that are dependent upon the specified dependency object.
- **DBMS_RESULT_CACHE.MEMORY_REPORT** -- produces a memory usage report for the Result Cache.

Client Result Cache

In addition to the server result cache, there is a new client result cache in 11G. The client-side result cache is completely separate from the server-side result cache. Unlike the server result cache, the OCI result cache does not cache results in the server SGA but rather in the memory of the client computer. The following server initialization parameters manager the client result cache:

- **CLIENT_RESULT_CACHE_SIZE** -- sets the memory allocated to the result cache. If you set the value to 0 (the default value), the result cache will be disabled.
- **CLIENT_RESULT_CACHE_LAG** -- sets the lag time for the client result cache. If the OCI application accesses the database infrequently, setting this parameter to a low value results in more round trips from the OCI client library to the database to keep the client result cache synchronized with the database.

Views

The following views provide information regarding the result cache:

- **V$RESULT_CACHE_STATISTICS** -- Lists the various cache settings and memory usage statistics.
- **V$RESULT_CACHE_MEMORY** -- Lists all the memory blocks and the corresponding statistics.
- **V$RESULT_CACHE_OBJECTS** -- Lists all the objects (cached results and dependencies) along with their attributes.
- **V$RESULT_CACHE_DEPENDENCY** -- Lists the dependency details between the cached results and dependencies.

Create temporary tablespace groups

Tablespace groups allow users to consume temporary space from multiple tablespaces. Tablespace groups can reduce problems caused when a single tablespace is inadequate to hold the results of a sort. Tablespace groups work particularly well on tables with many partitions because they enable parallel execution servers to use multiple temporary tablespaces. A tablespace group has the following characteristics:

- Contains at least one tablespace. There is no explicit maximum number of tablespaces that can be in a group.
- Shares the namespace of tablespaces, so its name cannot be the same as any tablespace.

- A tablespace group name can be specified wherever a tablespace name would appear when you assign a default temporary tablespace.

Creating a Tablespace Group

A tablespace group is created implicitly when you include the TABLESPACE GROUP clause in the CREATE TEMPORARY TABLESPACE or ALTER TABLESPACE statement and the specified tablespace group does not currently exist. If neither tsgroup1 nor tsgroup2 exists, then the following statements create those groups with the specified tablespace as the only member:

```
CREATE TEMPORARY TABLESPACE ocptemp1
TEMPFILE '/u02/oracle/data/ocptemp101.dbf'
SIZE 50M
TABLESPACE GROUP tsgroup1;

ALTER TABLESPACE ocptemp2 TABLESPACE GROUP tsgroup2;
```

Changing Members of a Tablespace Group

A tablespace can be added to an existing tablespace group by specifying the existing group name in a CREATE TEMPORARY TABLESPACE or ALTER TABLESPACE statement. The following example adds a tablespace to an existing group.

```
CREATE TEMPORARY TABLESPACE ocptemp3
TEMPFILE '/u02/oracle/data/ocptemp301.dbf'
SIZE 25M
TABLESPACE GROUP tsgroup1;
```

The following statement moves a tablespace to an existing group. Because tablespace ocptemp2 already belongs to ocpgroup2, it is moved from ocpgroup2 to ocpgroup1:

```
ALTER TABLESPACE ocptemp2
TABLESPACE GROUP tsgroup1;
```

Because this was the only tablespace in tsgroup2, that group has been implicitly deleted.

You can remove a tablespace from a group by supplying a null tablespace group in the TABLESPACE GROUP clause as follows::

```
ALTER TABLESPACE ocptemp2
TABLESPACE GROUP '';
```

Assign temporary tablespace groups to users

Tablespace groups can be used in the ALTER DATABASE...DEFAULT TEMPORARY TABLESPACE statement. This will assign the tablespace group as the default temporary tablespace for the database. The tablespace you assign or reassign as the default temporary tablespace must have a standard block size. An example of assigning a tablespace group as the default follows:

```
ALTER DATABASE ocp
DEFAULT TEMPORARY TABLESPACE ocpgroup1;
```

Any user who has not explicitly been assigned a temporary tablespace will now use the tablespaces in ocpgroup1. When a tablespace group has been specified as the default temporary tablespace, it is not possible to drop any of its member tablespaces. To remove members, you must first remove the tablespace from the tablespace group. Likewise, you cannot drop a single temporary tablespace as long as it is the default temporary tablespace.

Alternately, you can assign a tablespace group directly to users as their temporary tablespace using the ALTER USER command:

```
ALTER USER ocpuser
TEMPORARY TABLESPACE ocpgroup1;
```

Temporary Tablespace Enhancements

Shrinking Temporary Tablespaces

When large sort operations are performed by the database, they can result in a temporary tablespace growing and occupying a considerable amount of disk space. When the sort operation completes, the extra space does not get released automatically to the file system; it is just marked as free and available for reuse. An unusually large sort operation might create a temporary tablespace much larger than what is required for normal operations. In 11G, a new command enables you to shrink locally managed temporary tablespaces and release unused space. You use the SHRINK SPACE clause of the ALTER TABLESPACE statement to shrink a temporary tablespace, or the SHRINK TEMPFILE clause of the ALTER TABLESPACE statement to shrink a single file of a temporary tablespace. Shrinking frees the maximum space possible while maintaining the other attributes of the tablespace or tempfile. The optional KEEP clause defines a minimum size for the tablespace or tempfile.

```
ALTER TABLESPACE temp_ts1 SHRINK SPACE KEEP 30M;
```

DBA_TEMP_FREE_SPACE

The DBA_TEMP_FREE_SPACE dictionary view is new with Oracle 11G. It contains information about space usage for each temporary tablespace. The information includes the space allocated and the free space. You can query this view for these statistics using the following command.

```
SELECT * from DBA_TEMP_FREE_SPACE;
```

Global Temporary Tables

Prior to Oracle 11g, it was not possible to specify a tablespace when creating a global temporary table. In 11G, it is now possible to set the tablespace where the global temporary table will be created. If not specified, the temporary table will be created in the default temporary tablespace. This feature allows you to assign temporary tables to tablespaces with extent sizes appropriate for the use of that table. This, in turn, can lead to improved performance.

Oracle SecureFiles

Use Secure File LOBS to store documents with Compression, Encryption, De-duplication, Caching

SecureFile LOBs vs. BasicFile LOBs

In Oracle 11G, a new type of Large-Object storage has been added, SecureFile LOBs. The legacy LOB format has been renamed to BasicFile LOBs. SecureFile LOBs add several new capabilities to LOB data storage:

- Intelligent LOB compression enables users to explicitly compress data to save disk space.
- Intelligent LOB encryption allows encrypted data to be stored in-place and is available for random reads and writes.
- The deduplication option allows Oracle to automatically detect duplicate LOB data and conserve space by only storing a single copy of the data.
- LOB data path optimization includes logical cache above storage layer, read prefetching, new caching modes, vectored IO, and more.

db_securefile parameter

The new init.ora parameter, db_securefile, is used to determine the behavior of the Oracle database in reference to using or not using SecureFile LOBs or BasicFile LOBs. The possible values of this parameter are: ALWAYS, FORCE, PERMITTED, NEVER, and IGNORE. The meaning of each of the values is:

- **ALWAYS** -- attempt to create SecureFile LOBs but fall back to BasicFile LOBs if the tablespace is not using ASSM.
- **FORCE** -- force all LOBs created going forward to be SecureFile LOBs. If the LOB is being created in an MSSM tablespace, an error will be thrown.
- **PERMITTED** -- allow SecureFile LOBs to be created
- **NEVER** -- disallow SecureFile LOBs from being created. If a DML statement tries to create a column as a SecureFile LOB, it will instead be created as a BasicFile LOB. If any SecureFile specific

storage options or features are in the DML, an exception is created.

- **IGNORE** -- disallow SecureFile LOBs and ignore any errors that would otherwise be caused by forcing BasicFile LOBs with SecureFile options.

Migration to Secure File LOBs

Online redefinition is the only method Oracle recommends for migrating BasicFile LOBs to SecureFile LOBs. Online redefinition can be performed at the table or partition level. Using online redefinition means that the tables or partitions do not need to be taken offline. You can also perform the operation in parallel. However, the operation will require additional storage equal to the entire table or partition and all LOB segments. Also, after the migration, global indexes for the table will have to be rebuilt.

Use SQL and PL/SQL APIs to access Secure File LOBS

DBMS_LOB

SecureFiles inherit the LOB column settings for deduplication, encryption, and compression that were specified at the time the LOB was created. You can use the new procedures added to the DBMS_LOB package to determine or override the inherited values.

- **DBMS_LOB.GETOPTIONS** -- The current settings of a SecureFile LOB can be obtained using this function. An integer corresponding to a pre-defined constant based on the option type is returned. As an example, the value for DEDUPLICATE_OFF is 0. You won't need to know the values for the test. You might need to know the procedure name.
- **DBMS_LOB.SETOPTIONS** -- This procedure sets features of a SecureFile LOB (compression, deduplication, and encryption). It enables the features to be set on a per-LOB basis, overriding the default LOB settings.
- **DBMS_LOB.ISSECUREFILE** -- This function returns TRUE or FALSE depending on whether the LOB locator (BLOB or CLOB) passed to it is for a SecureFile.

DBMS_SPACE.SPACE_USAGE

The existing SPACE_USAGE procedure is overloaded to return information about LOB space usage. It returns the amount of disk space in blocks used by all the LOBs in the LOB segment. This procedure can only be used on tablespaces that are created with auto segment space management.

SQL Tuning

Use the SQL Tuning Advisor

As SQL statements are executed by the Oracle database, the query optimizer works to generate good execution plans for them. The query optimizer has two modes of operation: a normal mode and a tuning mode.

- **Normal mode** -- The optimizer compiles the SQL and generates an execution plan with sub-second time constraints during which it must find a good execution plan.
- **Tuning mode** -- The optimizer performs additional analysis to check whether the 'normal' execution plan can be improved upon. The output of the query optimizer in tuning mode is not an execution plan, but a series of actions, along with a rationale and expected benefit for producing a significantly superior plan.

When running in the tuning mode, the optimizer is referred to as the Automatic Tuning Optimizer. While running in tuning mode, the optimizer can take several minutes to tune a single statement. It's not practical to invoke the Automatic Tuning Optimizer every time a query has to be hard-parsed. It is meant to be used for complex and high-load SQL statements that have a negative impact on the database. The Automatic Tuning Optimizer performs four types of tuning analysis.

Statistics Analysis

Oracle's query optimizer makes use of object statistics to generate execution plans. When statistics are stale or missing, the optimizer can generate sub-optimal execution plans. The Automatic Tuning Optimizer checks for missing or stale statistics, and produces two types of output. The first is recommendations to gather statistics for objects where the statistics are stale or missing. The second type of statistics output is auxiliary information. This takes the form of statistics for objects with no statistics, and statistic adjustment factor for objects with stale statistics. This auxiliary information is stored in an object called a SQL Profile.

SQL Profiling

Sometimes the query optimizer produces inaccurate estimates about an attribute of a statement due to lack of information, leading to poor execution plans. This can sometimes be corrected by manually adding hints to the SQL in order to guide the optimizer into making better decisions. Hints are not always effective, are labor intensive, and are often impractical when using packaged applications. SQL profiling is intended to be a solution for this problem. The Automatic Tuning Optimizer stores additional data regarding the SQL statement called a SQL Profile. The profile consists of auxiliary statistics specific to that statement. A SQL Profile collects additional information using sampling and partial execution techniques to help the optimizer make decisions about cardinality and other traits of the SQL query. In addition, the Automatic Tuning Optimizer also uses execution history information of the SQL statement to appropriately set optimizer parameter settings in the profile. An accepted SQL Profile is stored persistently in the data dictionary. SQL Profiles are specific to the particular query they were created for. After accepting the profile, if that statement is executed in the database again, the optimizer uses normal statistics in addition to the profile data when generating an execution plan. The additional information makes it possible to produce well-tuned plans for the corresponding SQL statement without. A SQL Profile does not act like a stored outline to freeze the execution plan of a SQL statement. As changes happen to the tables against which the SQL is run, the execution plan can change with the same SQL Profile.

Access Path Analysis

The use of indexes can tremendously enhance performance of a SQL statement. Properly used, they can reduce the need for full table scans on large tables and speed up join operations when querying multiple tables. Adding indexes to tables is a common method to drop query times. One of the functions of the optimizer is to investigate whether a new index can significantly enhance the performance of a query. If it identifies the need for such an index, it recommends its creation. The Automatic Tuning Optimizer does not analyze how its index recommendation can affect the remainder of the SQL workload. It therefore also recommends running the SQL Access Advisor utility on the SQL statement along with a representative SQL workload. Unlike the Automatic Tuning Optimizer, the

SQL Access Advisor does look at the impact of creating an index on the entire SQL workload before making any recommendations.

SQL Structure Analysis

The Automatic Tuning Optimizer identifies common problems with the structure of SQL statements that can lead to poor performance. The structure issues could be syntactic, semantic, or design problems with the statement. Whatever the issue, Automatic Tuning Optimizer makes relevant suggestions to restructure the SQL statements. It will suggest an alternative that is similar, but not equivalent, to the original statement. For example, the optimizer may suggest replacing a UNION operator with a UNION ALL or to replace NOT IN with NOT EXISTS. The developer can then decide if the advice is applicable in the given situation. SQL structure changes require a deep understanding of the data properties and should be implemented only after considering all the implications.

Automatic SQL Tuning

The Automatic Tuning Optimizer runs as an automated task on high-load SQL statements identified by the AWR as tuning candidates. This task, called Automatic SQL Tuning, runs in the default maintenance windows on a nightly basis. By default, it will run for at most one hour during any given maintenance window and perform the following steps:

1. Identify SQL candidates in the AWR for tuning. Oracle uses data from the AWR to generate a list of potential SQL statements that are eligible for tuning. Candidates will typically be repeating high-load statements that have a significant impact on the system. Only statements that have an execution plan with a high potential for improvement will be marked for tuning. Recursive SQL and statements that have been tuned recently are ignored, as are parallel queries, DMLs, AND DDLs. The candidates are then ordered based on their performance impact. The performance impact of a SQL statement is calculated by summing the CPU time and the I/O times captured in the AWR for that SQL statement in the past week.
2. Each SQL statement is individually tuned by calling the SQL Tuning Advisor. During the tuning process, all recommendation types are considered and reported, but only SQL profiles can be implemented automatically.

3. Test SQL profiles by executing the SQL statement. If a SQL profile is recommended, the tuning advisor will execute the SQL statement with and without the profile.
4. Optionally implement the SQL profiles. Only if the performance improves at least threefold will the SQL profile be accepted automatically (and then only if the ACCEPT_SQL_PROFILES task parameter is set to TRUE). A profile will not be implemented if the objects referenced in the SQL statement have stale optimizer statistics. SQL profiles that have been implemented automatically will have their type set to AUTO in the DBA_SQL_PROFILES view.

SQL Access Advisor Overview

Optimizing access to data

Whereas SQL Tuning Advisor is designed to make sure that SQL statements are taking the most efficient path to provide the data requested, SQL Access Advisor is designed to help make sure that an efficient path to the data exists. SQL Access advisor offers recommendations intended to achieve the proper set of materialized views, materialized view logs, and indexes for a given workload. As a general rule, as the number of materialized views and indexes increase, query performance improves. SQL Access Advisor weighs trade-offs between space usage and query performance. SQL Access Advisor makes recommendations, each of which will contain one or more actions. If a recommendation contains multiple actions, all of the individual actions must be implemented to achieve the full benefit. If the Advisor decides that one or more base tables should be partitioned, it will collect all individual partition actions into a single recommendation. In that case, note that some or all of the remaining recommendations might be dependent on implementing the partitioning recommendation. It's not possible to view index and materialized view advice in isolation of the underlying table's partitioning.

Modes of Operation

SQL Access Advisor has two modes of operation: problem solving and evaluation. The default mode is problem solving. In this mode, SQL Access Advisor will attempt to solve access method problems by looking for new objects to create. When operating in evaluation mode, SQL Access Advisor will only comment on existing access paths that the given workload will use. A problem solving run might recommend creating a new index whereas an evaluation only scenario will only produce recommendations such as retaining an existing index. The evaluation mode is useful in determining which indexes and materialized views are actually being used by a given workload.

Intermediate Results

With 11G, SQL Access Advisor allows you to see intermediate results during the analysis operation. Previously, results were unavailable until the processing had completed or was interrupted by the user. With the change, it is possible to access results in the recommendation and action tables while the SQL Access Advisor task is still executing. Intermediate results represent recommendations only for the portion of the workload that has been executed up to that point in time. If the entire workload must be evaluated, then you should allow the task to complete normally. Recommendations made by the advisor early in the evaluation process will not have any base table partitioning recommendations. Partitioning analysis requires most of the workload to be processed before it's clear whether partitioning would be beneficial.

Create SQL Access Advisor analysis session using PL/SQL

Creating Tasks

You create advisor tasks to define what it is you want to analyze and where the analysis results should be placed. It's possible to create any number of tasks, each with a given specialization. All are based on the same Advisor task model and share the same repository. Tasks are created using the CREATE_TASK procedure:

```
VARIABLE task_id NUMBER;
VARIABLE task_name VARCHAR2(255);
EXECUTE :task_name := 'MYTASK';
EXECUTE DBMS_ADVISOR.CREATE_TASK ('SQL Access Advisor',
:task_id, :task_name);
```

SQL Tuning Sets

The input workload for the SQL Access Advisor is the SQL Tuning Set. An important benefit of using a SQL Tuning Set is that because SQL Tuning Sets are stored as separate entities, they can be referenced by many Advisor tasks. A workload reference will be removed when a parent Advisor task is deleted or when the workload reference is removed from the Advisor task by the user. A SQL Tuning Set workload is created using DBMS_SQLTUNE. You can pull SQL Workload objects into a SQL Tuning Set using DBMS_ADVISOR:

```
EXECUTE
DBMS_ADVISOR.COPY_SQLWKLD_TO_STS('MYWORKLOAD','MYSTS','NEW');
```

Linking Tasks and Workloads

Tasks must be linked to a SQL Tuning Set in order to generate advisor recommendations. You create links with the ADD_STS_REF procedure, using their respective names to link the task to a Tuning Set. Once a connection has been defined, the SQL Tuning Set is protected from removal or update.

```
EXECUTE DBMS_ADVISOR.ADD_STS_REF('MYTASK', null,
'MYWORKLOAD');
```

Removing a Link

Before a task or a SQL Tuning Set workload can be deleted, any existing links between the task and the workload must be removed. Links are removed using the DELETE_STS_REF procedure.

```
EXECUTE DBMS_ADVISOR.DELETE_STS_REF('MYTASK', null,
'MYWORKLOAD');
```

Recommendation Options

Parameters for a given task must be defined using the SET_TASK_PARAMETER procedure before recommendations can be generated. If parameters are not defined, then the defaults are used. You can set task parameters by using the SET_TASK_PARAMETER procedure.

```
DBMS_ADVISOR.SET_TASK_PARAMETER (
  task_name IN VARCHAR2,
  parameter IN VARCHAR2,
  value IN [VARCHAR2 | NUMBER]);
```

Generating Recommendations

You can generate recommendations by using the EXECUTE_TASK procedure. After it completes, the DBA_ADVISOR_LOG table will show execution status and the number of recommendations and actions produced. EXECUTE_TASK is a synchronous operation, so control will not be returned to the user until the operation has completed, or is interrupted. Upon completion, you can check the DBA_ADVISOR_LOG table for the execution status. The recommendations can be queried by task name in DBA_ADVISOR_RECOMMENDATIONS and the actions in DBA_ADVISOR_ACTIONS.

```
EXECUTE DBMS_ADVISOR.EXECUTE_TASK('MYTASK');
```

Setup and modify Automatic SQL Tuning

The behavior of the automatic SQL tuning task can be configured using the DBMS_SQLTUNE package. In order to use the APIs, the user needs to be granted at least the ADVISOR privilege. DBMS_SQLTUNE allows you to configure the standard behavior of the SQL Tuning Advisor, as well as configuring automatic SQL tuning. You do so by specifying the task parameters using the SET_TUNING_TASK_PARAMETER procedure. Because the automatic tuning task is owned by SYS, only the SYS user can set the task parameters for it.

```
BEGIN
  DBMS_SQLTUNE.SET_TUNING_TASK_PARAMETER(
         task_name  => 'SYS_AUTO_SQL_TUNING_TASK',
         parameter  => 'ACCEPT_SQL_PROFILES', value =>
'TRUE');
END;
```

- **ACCEPT_SQL_PROFILE** -- Specifies whether to accept SQL profiles automatically.
- **MAX_SQL_PROFILES_PER_EXEC** -- Specifies the limit of SQL profiles that are accepted for each automatic SQL tuning task.

- **MAX_AUTO_SQL_PROFILES** -- Specifies the limit of SQL profiles that are accepted in total.
- **EXECUTION_DAYS_TO_EXPIRE** -- Specifies the number of days for which to save the task history in the advisor framework schema. By default, the task history is saved for 30 days.

Interpret reports generated by Automatic SQL Tuning

You can use the DBMS_SQLTUNE.REPORT_AUTO_TUNING_TASK function to generate an automatic SQL tuning report. The report contains information about all executions of the automatic SQL tuning task. In order to run this report, you need the ADVISOR privilege and SELECT privileges on the DBA_ADVISOR views. The standard SQL tuning report generated using the DBMS_SQLTUNE.REPORT_TUNING_TASK function, contains information about a single task execution of the SQL Tuning Advisor. By contrast, the automatic SQL tuning report contains information about multiple executions of the automatic SQL tuning task. Depending on the sections that are included in a report, you can view the following information about the automatic SQL tuning task:

- **General information** -- provides a high-level description of the automatic SQL tuning task. It includes information about the inputs given for the report, the number of SQL statements tuned during the maintenance, and the number of SQL profiles that were created
- **Summary** -- lists the SQL statements that were tuned during the maintenance window and the estimated benefit of each SQL profile, or their actual execution statistics after test executing the SQL statement with the SQL profile
- **Tuning findings** -- contains the following information about each SQL statement analyzed by the SQL Tuning Advisor:
  - ✓ All findings associated with each SQL statement
  - ✓ Whether the profile was accepted on the system, and why
  - ✓ Whether the SQL profile is currently enabled on the system
  - ✓ Detailed execution statistics captured when testing the SQL profile

- **Explain plans** -- shows the old and new explain plans used by each SQL statement analyzed by the SQL Tuning Advisor.
- **Errors** -- lists all errors encountered by the automatic SQL tuning task.

SQL Tuning Information Views

- **DBA_ADVISOR_ACTIONS** -- displays information about the actions associated with all recommendations in the database.
- **DBA_ADVISOR_TASKS** -- displays information about all tasks in the database.
- **DBA_ADVISOR_EXECUTIONS** -- displays metadata information for task executions.
- **DBA_ADVISOR_FINDINGS** -- displays the findings discovered by all advisors in the database.
- **DBA_ADVISOR_RECOMMENDATIONS** -- displays the results of an analysis of all recommendations in the database.
- **DBA_ADVISOR_RATIONALE** -- displays information about the rationales for all recommendations in the database.
- **DBA_ADVISOR_SQLSTATS** -- displays execution statistics for the test-execution of different SQL plans during the advisor analysis.
- **DBA_ADVISOR_SQLPLANS** -- displays the different SQL execution plans generated as part of an advisor analysis.

Use SQL Repair Advisor

SRA Functionality

If a SQL statement fails with a critical error, the new SQL Repair Advisor may be able to repair the failed statement. When run against a failed statement, the advisor analyzes the statement to determine why it failed and can often recommend a patch to resolve the error. If applied, the SQL patch circumvents the failure by forcing the query optimizer to choose an alternate execution plan. SQL Repair Advisor is run from the Problem Details page of the Support Workbench in Oracle Enterprise Manager. What you'll need to know about SQL Repair advisor for the exam is that it is made to repair SQL statements that fail with a critical error. It is not made to tune functional statements. Also, implementing a patch does not change the SQL statement itself. The patch acts much like a SQL profile -- changing the execution plan chosen by the optimizer for the SQL statement as written.

Support Workbench

You can run the SQL Repair Advisor from the Problem Details page of the Support Workbench in Oracle Enterprise manager. If a SQL statement has failed with a critical error, a critical error will be present in the alerts section of OEM. The SQL Repair Advisor is available under the 'Problem Details' page for the displayed critical error.

DBMS_SQLDIAG

The SQL Repair Advisor can also be run by creating and executing a diagnostic task using the CREATE_DIAGNOSIS_TASK and EXECUTE_DIAGNOSIS_TASK of the SQLDIAG package. The SQL Repair Advisor reproduces the critical error and then tries to produce a SQL patch to work around the problem. The steps to diagnose and resolve a SQL patch are

1. Use DBMS_SQLDIAG.CREATE_DIAGNOSIS_TASK to create a new diagnosis task.
2. Use DBMS_SQLDIAG.EXECUTE_DIAGNOSIS_TASK with the task ID from step 1.
3. Use DBMS_SQLDIAG.REPORT_DIAGNOSIS_TASK to generate a report of the results.
4. Use DBMS_SQLDIAG.ACCEPT_SQL_PATCH to accept a patch.
5. Rerun the SQL statement to verify that it no longer fails.

Intelligent Infrastructure Enhancements

Monitor and maintain the AWR

The Automatic Workload Repository (AWR) collects database performance statistics. This data is both in memory and stored in the database and can be displayed in both reports and views. The statistics collected include:

- Object statistics that determine both access and usage statistics of database segments
- Time model statistics based on time usage for activities, displayed in the V$SYS_TIME_MODEL and V$SESS_TIME_MODEL views
- Some of the system and session statistics collected in the V$SYSSTAT and V$SESSTAT views
- SQL statements that are producing the highest load on the system, based on criteria such as elapsed time and CPU time
- ASH statistics, representing the history of recent session activity

*Active Session History

Gathering database statistics is controlled by the STATISTICS_LEVEL initialization parameter. STATISTICS_LEVEL should be set to TYPICAL (the default) or ALL to enable statistics gathering by the AWR. Setting STATISTICS_LEVEL to BASIC disables many Oracle Database features, including the AWR, and is not recommended.

Snapshots are sets of performance data for the database for a specific time periods. By default, Oracle generates snapshots once every hour and retains the statistics in the workload repository for 8 days. The data in the snapshot interval is then analyzed by the Automatic Database Diagnostic Monitor (ADDM). AWR compares snapshots to determine which SQL statements to capture based on their effect on system load. The primary interface for managing snapshots is Oracle Enterprise Manager. If Oracle Enterprise Manager is unavailable, you can manage snapshots using the DBMS_WORKLOAD_REPOSITORY package.

Automatic Workload Repository Views

AWR data is normally accessed via Oracle Enterprise Manager or AWR reports. However, you can also view it using the following views:

- V$**ACTIVE_SESSION_HISTORY** -- This view displays active database session activity, sampled once every second.
- **V$ metric views** -- Provide metric data to track the performance of the system. The metric views are organized into various groups, such as event, event class, system, session, service, file, and tablespace metrics. These groups are identified in the V$METRICGROUP view.
- **DBA_HIST_ACTIVE_SESS_HISTORY** -- Displays the history of the contents of the in-memory active session history for recent system activity
- **DBA_HIST_BASELINE** -- Displays information about the baselines captured on the system, such as the time range of each baseline and the baseline type
- **DBA_HIST_BASELINE_DETAILS** -- Displays details about a specific baseline
- **DBA_HIST_BASELINE_TEMPLATE** -- Displays information about the baseline templates used by the system to generate baselines
- **DBA_HIST_DATABASE_INSTANCE** -- Displays information about the database environment
- **DBA_HIST_DB_CACHE_ADVICE** -- Displays historical predictions of the number of physical reads for the cache size corresponding to each row
- **DBA_HIST_DISPATCHER** -- Displays historical information for each dispatcher process at the time of the snapshot
- **DBA_HIST_DYN_REMASTER_STATS** -- displays statistical information about the dynamic remastering process
- **DBA_HIST_IOSTAT_DETAIL** -- Displays historical I/O statistics aggregated by file type and function
- **DBA_HIST_SHARED_SERVER_SUMMARY** -- Displays historical information for shared servers, such as shared server activity, common queues and dispatcher queues
- **DBA_HIST_SNAPSHOT** -- Displays information on snapshots in the system
- **DBA_HIST_SQL_PLAN** -- Displays the SQL execution plans
- **DBA_HIST_WR_CONTROL** -- Displays the settings for controlling AWR

Generating Automatic Workload Repository Reports

An AWR report shows data captured between two selected snapshots. The report contains the workload profile of the system for the selected range of snapshots. You can generate AWR reports via Oracle Enterprise Manager or by running SQL scripts. The awrrpt.sql SQL script generates an HTML or text report that displays statistics for a range of snapshot IDs. To generate an AWR report:

1. At the SQL prompt, enter: @$ORACLE_HOME/rdbms/admin/awrrpt.sql
2. Specify whether you want an HTML or a text report:
3. Specify the number of days for which you want to list snapshot IDs.
4. Specify a beginning and ending snapshot ID for the workload repository report from the list of existing snapshots for the specified time range:
5. Enter a report name, or accept the default report name:

Creating and using AWR baselines

System-defined moving window baseline

An Oracle baseline contains performance data from a specific time period. It's used for comparison with other similar workload periods to troubleshoot performance problems. AWR snapshots in a baseline are excluded from the automatic purging process and are retained indefinitely.

- A fixed baseline corresponds to a fixed, contiguous time period in the past.
- A moving window baseline uses all of the data in the AWR retention period.
- A baseline template allows you to create baselines for a time period in the future.

Fixed baselines are useful for tracking performance changes over extended periods of time. Moving window baselines are useful when using adaptive thresholds because the data in the entire AWR retention period can be used to compute threshold values. Oracle automatically maintains a system-defined moving window baseline. The default window size for the system-defined moving window baseline is the current AWR retention period, which by default is 8 days. Consider using a larger moving window—such as 30 days if you are planning to use adaptive thresholds. A larger period will more accurately compute threshold values. To increase the size of a moving window, you must first increase the AWR retention period. In order to make use of thresholds, the baseline window size must be eight days or greater.

```
BEGIN
  DBMS_WORKLOAD_REPOSITORY.MODIFY_BASELINE_WINDOW_SIZE (
     window_size => 14);
END;
```

AWR Baseline Enhancements

Baseline templates schedule a baseline to be created for a contiguous time period in the future. It's possible to create single and repeating baseline templates.

A single baseline template is used to create a baseline for a single contiguous time period in the future. They can be used if you know of an event in the future that you want to capture metrics for. A repeating baseline template is used to create and drop baselines on a repeating schedule. This is used when you want Oracle to capture a contiguous time period multiple times.

There are two types of adaptive thresholds:

- **Percentage of maximum**: The threshold value is computed as a percentage multiple of the maximum value observed for the data in the moving window baseline.
- **Significance level**: The threshold value is set to a statistical percentile that represents how unusual it is to observe values above the threshold value based the data in the moving window baseline. The significance levels are:

✓ **High (.95)**: Only 5 in 100 observations are expected to exceed this value.

✓ **Very High (.99)**: Only 1 in 100 observations are expected to exceed this value.

✓ **Severe (.999)**: Only 1 in 1,000 observations are expected to exceed this value.

✓ **Extreme (.9999)**: Only 1 in 10,000 observations are expected to exceed this value.

There are several new procedures in DBMS_WORKLOAD_REPOSITORY to support the baseline functionality.

- **CREATE_BASELINE**: Creates a single baseline
- **CREATE_BASELINE_TEMPLATE**: Creates a baseline template
- **DROP_BASELINE**: Drops a range of snapshots
- **DROP_BASELINE_TEMPLATE**: Removes a baseline template that is no longer needed
- **MODIFY_BASELINE_WINDOW_SIZE**: Modifies the size for the Default Moving Window Baseline
- **RENAME_BASELINE**: Renames a baseline
- **SELECT_BASELINE_METRICS**: Shows the values of the metrics corresponding to a baseline

Setting AWR Baseline Metric Thresholds

Oracle Enterprise Manager is used to set baseline metric thresholds. Without a simulator the steps for this process from a testing standpoint are meaningless. You need to understand how the four Threshold settings apply to baselines.

- **Threshold Type** – Can be Percentage of Maximum or Significance Level.
- **Critical** – If the type is Percentage of Maximum, this would be set to a percentage. Otherwise, it would be one of the significance levels (High, Very High, Severe, Extreme).
- **Warning** – Same as with Critical, except (presumably) less extreme values.
- **Occurrences** – The number of occurrences required to trip the threshold.

Control Automated Maintenance Tasks

Oracle has automated tasks that are executed at regular intervals to perform maintenance operations on the system. Automated maintenance tasks are run during predefined maintenance windows on your database. Maintenance windows are predefined time intervals that are intended to occur during a period of low system load. Maintenance windows can be customized to fit the resource usage patterns of your database. You can also disable some or all of the default windows from running or create your own maintenance windows.

Oracle 11G has three predefined automated maintenance tasks that are configured to run in all maintenance windows by default:

- **Automatic Optimizer Statistics Collection** - This task collects optimizer statistics for all schema objects in the database for which there are no statistics or only stale statistics. The statistics are used by the SQL query optimizer to improve the performance of SQL execution.
- **Automatic Segment Advisor** - This task identifies segments that have space available for reclamation, and makes recommendations on how to defragment those segments.
- **Automatic SQL Tuning Advisor** - This task is new with Oracle 11G. It examines the performance of high-load SQL statements, and makes recommendations, along with a rationale for each recommendation and its expected benefit. The recommendation relates to: collection of statistics on objects; creation of new indexes; restructuring of the SQL statement; or creation of a SQL Profile. The only recommendation that the Automatic SQL Tuning Advisor can implement automatically is adding a SQL profile.

Predefined Maintenance Windows

Oracle 11G has seven predefined maintenance windows, one for each day of the week. The weekday windows run four hours – 10:00pm to 2:00am. The weekend windows run 20 hours, 6:00am through 2:00AM the following day. As mentioned earlier, you can change or disable any of the predefined windows or add one or more of your own. During long maintenance windows, all automated maintenance tasks except Automatic SQL Tuning Advisor are restarted every four hours. This ensures that maintenance tasks are run regularly, regardless of window size.

```
MONDAY_WINDOW    10P Monday ->    2AM Tuesday
TUESDAY_WINDOW   10P Tuesday ->   2AM Wednesday
WEDNESAY_WINDOW  10P Wednesday -> 2AM Thursday
THURSDAY_WINDOW  10P Thursday ->  2AM Friday
FRIDAY_WINDOW    10P Friday ->    2AM Saturday
SATURDAY_WINDOW  6A  Saturday ->  2AM Sunday
SUNDAY_WINDOW    6A  Sunday ->    2AM Monday
```

Autotask Background Process (ABP)

In Oracle Database 11g, the new Auto-Task background process can run hundreds or thousands of jobs in the manageability windows. It interfaces with the Oracle scheduler to manage the job load imposed by the automated maintenance tasks. ABP provides out-of-the-box management of resource distribution (CPU and I/O) among the various database maintenance tasks. CPU load is automatically managed. I/O is managed only if the I/O Resource Manager is enabled. ABP ensures that the operation of the database during maintenance operations is not adversely affected and that user activity gets the necessary resources to complete.

The ABP process is started at the beginning of each maintenance window by MMON. Once started, it converts tasks into scheduler jobs for execution. The jobs are assigned using three priority levels: urgent, high, and medium. The ABP uses these priority levels when assigning tasks to consumer groups in the DEFAULT_MAINTENANCE_PLAN. ABP maintains History in the SYSAUX tablespace of all automated maintenance task executions. You can view this repository using the DBA_AUTOTASK_TASK view.

Disabling a Maintenance Task

By default, all maintenance tasks run in all predefined maintenance windows. It's possible to disable a maintenance task for a specific window using the DISABLE procedure OF THE DBMS_AUTO_TASK_ADMIN package. The following example disables the Automatic SQL Tuning Advisor from running in the window FRIDAY_WINDOW:

```
BEGIN
  DBMS_AUTO_TASK_ADMIN.DISABLE(
  client_name => 'sql tuning advisor',
  operation => NULL,
  window_name => 'FRIDAY_WINDOW');
END;
```

To disable the job in all windows, you would pass a NULL to the window_name parameter:

```
BEGIN
  DBMS_AUTO_TASK_ADMIN.DISABLE(
  client_name => 'sql tuning advisor',
  operation => NULL,
  window_name => NULL);
END;
```

Enabling a Maintenance Task

To enable this maintenance task in a single window, use the ENABLE procedure, as follows:

```
BEGIN
  dbms_auto_task_admin.enable(
  client_name => 'sql tuning advisor',
  operation => NULL,
  window_name => 'FRIDAY');
END;
```

And to enable the SQL Tuning Advisor in all windows, pass a NULL to the window_name parameter:

```
BEGIN
  dbms_auto_task_admin.enable(
  client_name => 'sql tuning advisor',
  operation => NULL,
  window_name => NULL);
END;
```

Using Database Resource Manager New Features

The Oracle Database Resource Manager (DRM) is designed to optimize resource allocation among concurrent database sessions. It attempts to prevent problems that can happen if the operating system makes resource decisions when presented with high overhead without having awareness of the database needs. DRM helps to overcome these problems by giving the database more control over how hardware resources are allocated. DRM enables you to classify sessions into groups based on session attributes, and then allocate resources to those groups in a way that optimizes hardware utilization for your application environment. The information that performs the functions of classifying sessions and assigning resources is called a resource plan. Oracle 11G comes with sophisticated new built-in resource plans for DRM. There is a mixed-workload plan that provides resource management for a mixed environment consisting of both OLTP and DSS/batch jobs. There is a Data Warehouse plan that provides resource management for a data warehousing environment. Finally there is the maintenance plan that provides resource management for the maintenance window. These plans are shipped with Oracle 11G and provide resource management directives that should provide immediate benefits for the majority of database installations. There are three elements of DRM:

- **Resource consumer group**: A group of sessions that are grouped together based on resource requirements.
- **Resource plan**: A container for directives that specify how resources are allocated to resource consumer groups.
- **Resource plan directive**: Associates a resource consumer group with a particular plan and specifies how resources are to be allocated to that resource consumer group.

Resource Plan Directives

A resource plan directive for a consumer group, can specify limits for CPU and I/O resource consumption for sessions in that group. This is done by specifying the action to be taken if a call within a session exceeds one of the specified limits. These actions, called switches, occur only for sessions that are running and consuming resources, not waiting for user input or for CPU cycles. The possible actions are the following:

- The session is switched to a consumer group with lower resource allocations.
- The session is killed (terminated).
- The session's current SQL statement is aborted.

The resource plan directive attribute that determines which of the above three actions will be taken is SWITCH_GROUP. This attribute specifies the consumer group to which a session is switched if the specified criteria are met. If the value of this parameter is a consumer group, the session will be switched to that group. If the group name is 'CANCEL_SQL', the current call for that session is canceled. Finally, if the group name is 'KILL_SESSION', then the session is killed.

Per session I/O or CPU Limits

The resource plan directive attributes that can be used in specifying the criteria to use in making switch determinations follow. If not set, all default to UNLIMITED.

- **SWITCH_TIME**: Specifies the time (in CPU seconds) that a call can execute before an action is taken.

- **SWITCH_IO_MEGABYTES**: Specifies the number of megabytes of I/O that a session can transfer (read and write) before being switched.
- **SWITCH_IO_REQS**: Specifies the number of I/O requests that a session can execute before an action is taken.

Be sure you understand the meaning of and difference between the two criteria for the test.

SWITCH_ESTIMATE and SWITCH_FOR_CALL
These two resource plan attributes can be used to modify the behavior of resource plan switching:

- **SWITCH_ESTIMATE**: If TRUE, the database estimates the execution time of each call. If the estimated execution time exceeds SWITCH_TIME, the session is moved to the SWITCH_GROUP before beginning the call. The default is FALSE.
- **SWITCH_FOR_CALL**: If TRUE, a session that was automatically switched to another consumer group is returned to its original consumer group when the top level call completes. The default is NULL.

Simplify management tasks by using the Scheduler

The Oracle Scheduler is implemented by the procedures and functions in the DBMS_SCHEDULER package. The Scheduler enables you to control when and where various tasks occur. The Scheduler provides sophisticated, flexible enterprise scheduling functionality, which you can use to:

- **Run database program units** -- You can run PL/SQL anonymous blocks, PL/SQL stored procedures, and Java stored procedures on the local database or on remote Oracle databases.
- **Run external executables** -- You can run applications, shell scripts, and batch files, on the local system or on one or more remote systems.

- **Schedule job execution using multiple methods** -- The scheduled can employ time-based scheduling, event-based scheduling, and dependency scheduling.
- **Prioritize jobs based on business requirements** -- The Scheduler provides control over resource allocation among competing jobs.
- **Manage and monitor jobs** -- You can track information such as the status of the job and the last run time of the job by querying views using Enterprise Manager or SQL.
- **Execute and manage jobs in a clustered environment** -- The Scheduler fully supports execution of jobs in a Real Application Cluster environment.

To use the Scheduler, you create Scheduler objects. Schema objects define the what, when, and where for job scheduling. Scheduler objects enable a modular approach to managing tasks. One advantage of the modular approach is that objects can be reused when creating new tasks that are similar to existing tasks.

The principal Scheduler object is the job. A job defines the action to perform, the schedule for the action, and the location or locations where the action takes place. Most other scheduler objects are created to support jobs.

Some key points about the Oracle Scheduler:

- You may run PL/SQL and Java stored procedure, C functions, regular SQL scripts, and UNIX or Windows scripts.
- You can create time-based or event-based jobs. Events can be application generated or scheduler-generated.
- The Scheduler consists of the concepts: Program, Job, Schedule, Job class, Resource group, Window and Window Group.
- The Scheduler architecture consists primarily of the job table, job coordinator, and the job workers (or slaves).

Create a job, program, schedule and window

There are multiple elements of the Scheduler architecture. All except jobs are optional.

- **Programs** -- The scheduler allows you to optionally create programs which hold metadata about a task, but no schedule information. A program may relate to a PL/SQL block, a stored procedure or an OS executable file. Programs are created using the CREATE_PROGRAM procedure.
- **Schedules** -- Schedules optionally define the start time, end time and interval related to a job.
- **Jobs** -- Jobs can either be made up of predefined parts (programs and schedules) or completely self contained depending on which overload of the CREATE_JOB procedure is used to create them.
- **Job Classes** -- Job classes allow grouping of jobs with similar characteristics and resource requirements which eases administration.
- **Windows** -- Windows provide the link between the scheduler and the resource manager, allowing different resource plans to be activated at different times.
- **Window Groups** -- A window group is a collection of related windows.

Creating Jobs

```
DBMS_SCHEDULER.CREATE_JOB(
  JOB_NAME        => 'TEST_JOB1',
  JOB_TYPE        => 'PLSQL_BLOCK',
  JOB_ACTION      => 'BEGIN mytestproc; END;',
  START_DATE      => SYSTIMESTAMP,
  REPEAT_INTERVAL => 'FREQ=DAILY;INTERVAL=2',
  END_DATE        => NULL,
  COMMENTS        => 'TEST JOB')
```

- **JOB_TYPE** -- Possible values are: plsql_block, stored_procedure, executable

- **JOB_ACTION** -- Specifies the exact procedure, command, or script that the job will execute.
- **START_DATE and END_DATE** -- Specify the date that a new job should start and end. (Many jobs may not have an end_date parameter)
- **REPEAT_INTERVAL** -- You can specify a repeat interval using a PL/SQL date/time expression or a database calendaring expression.
- **COMMENTS** -- Allows you to add descriptive text to the job.

Enabling and Disabling Jobs

All jobs are disabled by default when you create them. You must explicitly enable them in order to activate and schedule them. The following examples show how to enable and disable a job.

```
DBMS_SCHEDULER.ENABLE ('TEST_JOB1')

DBMS_SCHEDULER.DISABLE ('TEST_JOB1')
```

Creating a Program

A program describes what is to be run by the Scheduler and is a separate entity from a job. A job runs at a certain time or because a certain event occurred, and calls a program. Different jobs can use the same program and run the program at different times and with different settings.

```
DBMS_SCHEDULER.CREATE_PROGRAM(
  PROGRAM_NAME   => 'UPDATE_STATS',
  PROGRAM_ACTION => 'OCPUSER.UPDATE_SCHEMA_STATS',
  PROGRAM_TYPE   => 'STORED_PROCEDURE',
  ENABLED        => TRUE)
```

Once a program exists, it a job can be created using the program component as follows:

```
DBMS_SCHEDULER.CREATE_JOB(
JOB_NAME         => 'TEST_JOB1',
PROGRAM_NAME     => 'UPDATE_STATS',
REPEAT_INTERVAL=> 'FREQ=DAILY;BYHOUR=03',
ENABLED          => TRUE)
```

Creating a Schedule

A schedule object specifies when and how many times a job is run. Schedules can be shared by multiple jobs. When you create a schedule, Oracle provides access to PUBLIC. Thus, all users can use your schedule, without any explicit grant of privileges to do so. You specify the start and end times using the TIMESTAMP WITH TIME ZONE data type. The Scheduler also supports all NLS_TIMESTAMP_TZ_FORMAT settings. You must use a calendaring expression to create the repeat interval.

```
DBMS_SCHEDULER.CREATE_SCHEDULE(
  SCHEDULE_NAME    => 'SCHEDULE_12HR',
  START_DATE       => SYSTIMESTAMP,
  END_DATE         => NULL,
  REPEAT_INTERVAL  => 'FREQ=HOURLY;INTERVAL= 12',
  COMMENTS         => 'EVERY 12 HOURS')


DBMS_SCHEDULER.CREATE_JOB(
  JOB_NAME       => 'TEST_JOB02',
  PROGRAM_NAME   => 'UPDATE_STATS',
  SCHEDULE_NAME  => 'SCHEDULE_12HR')
```

Creating a Window

Windows link the scheduler to the resource manager, allowing different resource plans to be activated at different times. Since job classes point to resource consumer groups, and therefore resource plans, this mechanism allows control over the resources allocated to job classes and their jobs during specific time periods.

```
DBMS_SCHEDULER.create_window (
  window_name      => 'test_window_1',
  resource_plan    => NULL,
  schedule_name    => 'SCHEDULE_12HR',
  duration         => INTERVAL '60' MINUTE,
  window_priority => 'LOW',
  comments         => 'Window with a predefined schedule.');
```

View information about job executions and job instances

The job log contains information about job runs, job state changes, and job failures. Results for both local and remote jobs are available. The data dictionary views *_SCHEDULER_JOB_LOG and *_SCHEDULER_JOB_RUN_DETAILS allow access to the log.

Depending on the logging level that is in effect,

The Scheduler can make job log entries whenever a job is run and when a job is created, dropped, enabled, and more. For repeating jobs, the Scheduler makes one entry in the log for each job instance. Each log entry provides information about a particular run, such as the job completion status.

The following example shows job log entries for a repeating job that has run twice:

```
SELECT job_name, operation, status
FROM   user_scheduler_job_log;

JOB_NAME     OPERATION  STATUS
----------- ---------- -----------
OCPJOB       RUN        SUCCEEDED
OCPJOB       RUN        SUCCEEDED
```

The logging_level attribute of either a job or a job class controls how frequently information is written to the job log. Log entries for job runs are made when the job run completes successfully, fails, or is stopped. The following example shows job log entries for a complete job lifecycle when logging is set to LOGGING_FULL:

```
SELECT TO_CHAR(log_date, 'DD-MON HH24:MI:SS') TIMESTAMP,
       job_name, operation, status
FROM   user_scheduler_job_log
WHERE job_name = 'OCPJOB2'
ORDER BY log_date;

TIMESTAMP        JOB_NAME   OPERATION   STATUS
---------------- ---------  ----------  ---------
11-MAY 13:20:46 OCPJOB2     CREATE
11-MAY 13:22:05 OCPJOB2     UPDATE
11-MAY 13:22:21 OCPJOB2     ENABLE
11-MAY 13:22:51 OCPJOB2     RUN         SUCCEEDED
11-MAY 13:23:22 OCPJOB2     ENABLE
11-MAY 13:23:38 OCPJOB2     RUN         STOPPED
11-MAY 13:29:56 OCPJOB2     DROP
```

Run Details

For rows in *_SCHEDULER_JOB_LOG for RUN, RETRY_RUN, or RECOVERY_RUN operations, there will be a detail record in the *_SCHEDULER_JOB_RUN_DETAILS view. The views can be joined using the LOG_ID columns to match up the corresponding rows. The run details view is useful in determining why a job failed or was stopped. The details view also contains the job start time and duration.

```
SELECT TO_CHAR(log_date, 'DD-MON HH24:MI:SS') TIMESTAMP,
       status,
       SUBSTR(additional_info, 1, 40) ADDITIONAL_INFO
FROM   user_scheduler_job_run_details
WHERE  job_name = 'OCPJOB2'
ORDER BY log_date;

TIMESTAMP        STATUS    ADDITIONAL_INFO
---------------- --------- --------------------------------
11-MAY 13:22:51 SUCCEEDED
11-MAY 13:23:38 STOPPED    REASON="Stop job called by
                           user:'OCPUSER'
```

Job State Events

Jobs can be configured to trigger an event when the job changes state. Events can be raised when a job starts, completes, exceeds its allotted run time, and more. An application must accept these events and use them to trigger some action.

E-mail Notifications

Alternately, jobs can be configured to send e-mail notifications on state changes. Notifications can be sent to one or more recipients, and can be triggered by multiple events that you specify. It's also possible to create filter conditions that must be met in order to generate notifications. You must set the Scheduler attribute email_server to the address of the SMTP server before email notifications can be sent. Optionally you can set the Scheduler attribute email_sender to use a default sender e-mail address when jobs do not specify a sender.

Monitor and manage server-generated alerts

Server-generated alerts are designed to notify administrators of an impending problem. Notifications may also suggest a way to correct the problem. The server can also provide notifications condition has been cleared. The server creates alerts when a problem occurs or when data does not match expected values for metrics, such as Physical Reads Per Second, User Commits Per Second, or SQL Service Response Time.

Server-generated alerts can be based on events or thresholds. Threshold alerts can be triggered at warning and critical levels. Some alerts have default threshold levels which can be changed if desired. Oracle has a default alert for tablespace space usage when the percentage used exceeds either the 85% warning or 97% critical threshold level. Examples of event based alerts are: Snapshot Too Old and Resumable Session Suspended.

Viewing Alerts

Alerts are displayed on the Enterprise Manager Database Home page and can be configured to send email or pager notifications as well. If an alert cannot be written to the alert queue, a message about the alert is written to the Oracle Database alert log. To use a custom tool to display alerts, you must subscribe to the ALERT_QUE, read the ALERT_QUE, and display an alert notification after setting the threshold levels for an alert. The CREATE_AQ_AGENT and ADD_SUBSCRIBER procedures of the

DBMS_AQADM package can be used to create an agent and subscribe the agent to the ALERT_QUE. You must also associate a database user with the subscribing agent. This allows the user to access queued messages in the secure ALERT_QUE. The user must also be assigned enqueue privilege with the ENABLE_DB_ACCESS and GRANT_QUEUE_PRIVILEGE procedures of the DBMS_AQADM package.

Server-Generated Alerts Data Dictionary Views

The following data dictionary views provide information about server-generated alerts.

- **DBA_THRESHOLDS** -- Lists the threshold settings defined for the instance
- **DBA_OUTSTANDING_ALERTS** -- Describes the outstanding alerts in the database
- **DBA_ALERT_HISTORY** -- Lists a history of alerts that have been cleared
- **V$ALERT_TYPES** -- Provides information such as group and type for each alert
- **V$METRICNAME** -- Contains the names, identifiers, and other information about the system metrics
- **V$METRIC** -- Contains system-level metric values
- **V$METRIC_HISTORY** -- Contains a history of system-level metric values

Performance Enhancements

Use Automatic Database Diagnostic Monitor (ADDM)

The Automatic Workload Repository (AWR) captures and stores the statistical data needed to diagnose problems with the database. The Automatic Database Diagnostic Monitor (ADDM) makes use of this data to perform that diagnosis. Automatic database diagnostic monitoring is controlled by the CONTROL_MANAGEMENT_PACK_ACCESS and the STATISTICS_LEVEL initialization parameters. The CONTROL_MANAGEMENT_PACK_ACCESS parameter should be set to DIAGNOSTIC or DIAGNOSTIC+TUNING (the default) to enable automatic database diagnostic monitoring. Setting CONTROL_MANAGEMENT_PACK_ACCESS to NONE disables ADDM. The STATISTICS_LEVEL parameter should be set to the TYPICAL (the default) or ALL to enable automatic database diagnostic monitoring. Setting STATISTICS_LEVEL to BASIC disables ADDM. ADDM performs the following functions:

- Analyzes the AWR data on a regular basis
- Diagnoses the root causes of performance problems
- Provides recommendations for correcting any problems
- Identifies non-problem areas of the system

ADDM Analysis

An ADDM analysis can be performed on a pair of AWR snapshots and a set of instances from the same database. The pair of AWR snapshots define the time period for analysis, and the set of instances define the target for analysis. ADDM has three analysis modes, of which only 'Instance' is applicable is you are not in a RAC environment:

- **Database** -- In Database mode, ADDM analyzes all instances of the database.
- **Instance** -- In Instance mode, ADDM analyzes a particular instance of the database.
- **Partial** -- In Partial mode, ADDM analyzes a subset of all database instances.

Oracle performs an ADDM analysis every time an AWR snapshot is taken and saves the results in the database. The time period analyzed by ADDM is determined by the time between the last two snapshots. Once the analysis is complete, you can view the results in Oracle Enterprise Manager, or by viewing a report in a SQL*Plus session.

Diagnosing Database Performance Problems with ADDM

Review the ADDM analysis results that are automatically created each time an AWR snapshot is taken. If a different analysis is required, you can run ADDM manually. ADDM does not have to analyze the last two snapshots. It can make use of any pair of snapshots on the same database so long as both are after the most recent startup of the database. Oracle recommends running ADDM using Oracle Enterprise Manager. If this is not possible, you can run ADDM using the DBMS_ADDM package. In order to run the DBMS_ADDM APIs, the user must be granted the ADVISOR privilege.

To analyze a particular instance of the database, you can run ADDM in Instance mode. To run ADDM in Instance mode, use the DBMS_ADDM.ANALYZE_INST procedure:

```
BEGIN
  DBMS_ADDM.ANALYZE_INST (
    task_name IN OUT VARCHAR2,
    begin_snapshot IN NUMBER,
    end_snapshot IN NUMBER,
    instance_number IN NUMBER := NULL,
    db_id IN NUMBER := NULL);
END;
/
```

- **task_name** -- Specifies the name of the analysis task that will be created.
- **begin_snapshot** -- Specifies the snapshot number of the beginning snapshot in the analysis period.
- **end_snapshot** -- Specifies the snapshot number of the ending snapshot in the analysis period.
- **instance_number** -- Specifies the instance number of the instance that will be analyzed.

- **db_id** -- Specifies the database identifier of the database that will be analyzed. If unspecified, this parameter defaults to the database identifier of the database to which you are currently connected.

The following example creates an ADDM task in instance analysis mode, and executes it to diagnose the performance of instance number 1 during the time period defined by snapshots 247 and 252:

```
DECLARE
  V_task VARCHAR2(30);
BEGIN
  V_task := 'Example ADDM';
  DBMS_ADDM.ANALYZE_INST(v_task, 247, 252, 1);
END;
/
```

Displaying an ADDM Report

To display a text report of an executed ADDM task, use the DBMS_ADDM.GET_REPORT function. The return type of GET_REPORT is a CLOB, formatted to fit a line size of 80. The following example displays a text report of the ADDM task specified by its task name:

```
SET LONG 1000000 PAGESIZE 0;
SELECT DBMS_ADDM.GET_REPORT('Example ADDM') FROM dual;
```

ADDM Enhancements in 11g

Real Application Clusters

ADDM has been enhanced to provide performance diagnostic and tuning advice for all nodes in a Real Application Cluster. A new mode of ADDM analyzes an Oracle RAC database and reports issues that affect the entire cluster in addition to those that are affecting individual instances. The new capability is of particular use for global resources such as interconnect traffic and I/O. It simplifies the task of tuning RAC databases and makes the results more precise. When using ADDM in a RAC database, you have the option of running it in any of three modes:

- **Database** -- Provides metrics for the entire cluster.
- **Instance** -- Provides metrics for a single instance.
- **Partial** -- Provides metrics for more than one, but not all nodes in the cluster.

DBMS_ADDM Package
Oracle suggests using Oracle Enterprise Manager as the primary interface for diagnostic monitoring. However, it's also possible to run ADDM using the DBMS_ADDM package. In order to run the DBMS_ADDM APIs, the user must be granted the ADVISOR privilege.

- **DBMS_ADDM.ANALYZE_DB** - Run ADDM in Database Mode.
- **DBMS_ADDM.ANALYZE_INST** - Run ADDM in Instance Mode.
- **DBMS_ADDM.ANALYZE_PARTIAL** - Run ADDM in Partial Mode.
- **SELECT DBMS_ADDM.GET_REPORT(:task_name) FROM DUAL;** - Display an ADDM Report.

Findings and Directives
ADDM analysis results are represented as a set of findings. Findings come in four classes:

- **Problem** findings describe the root cause of a database performance problem.
- **Symptom** findings contain information that often leads to one or more problem findings.
- **Information** findings report information that provides background data, but does not constitute a performance problem.
- **Warning** findings contain information about problems that may affect the accuracy of the ADDM analysis.

Directives alter the recommendations provided by ADDM, by filtering the result set or eliminating certain finding types altogether. The DBMS_ADDM package has several INSERT...DIRECTIVE procedures:

- **INSERT_FINDING_DIRECTIVE** - Limit reporting of a specific finding type.
- **INSERT_PARAMETER_DIRECTI**VE - Prevents ADDM from creating actions to alter the value of a specific system parameter
- **INSERT_SEGMENT_DIRECTIVE** - Prevents ADDM from creating actions to "run Segment Advisor" for specific segments
- **INSERT_SQL_DIRECTIVE** - Creates a directive to limit reporting of actions on specific SQL

Each of the INSERT...DIRECTIVE procedures has a corresponding DELETE...DIRECTIVE procedure that removes a directive thus created.

New Views

You can locate ADDM information through the DBA_ADVISOR views:

- **DBA_ADVISOR_FINDINGS** - Displays all the findings discovered by all advisors.
- **DBA_ADVISOR_FINDING_NAMES** - List of all finding names registered with the advisor framework.
- **DBA_ADVISOR_RECOMMENDATIONS** - Displays the results of completed diagnostic tasks with recommendations for the problems identified in each execution.
- **DBA_ADVISOR_TASKS** - Provides basic information about existing tasks, such as the task ID, task name, and when the task was created.

Use Automatic Shared Memory Management

Automatic memory management enables Oracle Database to automatically manage and tune all aspects of the instance memory. Using automatic memory management requires only one parameter to be set (although there is one optional parameter).

- **MEMORY_TARGET** -- The target memory size initialization parameter
- **MEMORY_MAX_TARGET** -- A maximum memory size initialization parameter (optional).

When the MEMORY_TARGET parameter is set, the database tunes to the target memory size, redistributing memory as needed between the system global area (SGA) and the instance program global area (instance PGA). Oracle strongly recommends the use of automatic memory management to manage the memory on your system.

Setup Automatic Memory Management

The new memory_target parameter is the only value that needs to be set to allow Oracle to automatically manage memory. You need to understand what it does, and how the four parameters below relate to each other when set (or not set).

memory_target
When MEMORY_TARGET is set, the database will allocate this much memory on startup, by default granting 60% to the SGA and 40% to the PGA. Over time, as the database runs, it will redistribute memory as needed between the system global area (SGA) and the instance program global area (instance PGA). If MEMORY_TARGET is not set, automatic memory management is not enabled, even if you have set a value for MEMORY_TARGET_MAX.

memory_target_max
When set, this determines the maximum amount of memory that Oracle will grab from the OS for the SGA and PGA. If this value is not set, it will default to the MEMORY_TARGET value.

sga_target
This value is not required if using automatic memory management. If this value is set and MEMORY_TARGET is also set, then the value of SGA_TARGET becomes the minimum amount of memory allocated to the SGA by automatic memory management.

pga_aggregate_target
This value is not required if using automatic memory management. If this value is set and MEMORY_TARGET is also set, then the value of PGA_AGGREGATE_TARGET becomes the minimum amount of memory allocated to the PGA by automatic memory management.

Enhancements in statistics collection

Pending Statistics
Starting with the 11g Release, it's possible to automatically publish the statistics at the end of the gather operation (the default behavior), or to have the new statistics saved as pending. When saved as pending, you can validate the new statistics and publish them only if they generate

acceptable optimizer plans. The command SELECT DBMS_STATS.GET_PREFS('PUBLISH') publish from dual; will return 'TRUE' if statistics will be published when they are gathered, or FALSE if the statistics will be kept pending. You can change the PUBLISH setting at either the schema or the table level. By default, the optimizer uses only published statistics in generating plans. If you want the optimizer to use pending statistics, you may set the initialization parameter OPTIMIZER_USE_PENDING_STATISTICS to TRUE (the default value is FALSE). You may publish pending stats for a single table, single schema, or the entire database with the DBMS_STATS.PUBLISH_PENDING_STATS procedure;

- **Database** - DBMS_STATS.PUBLISH_PENDING_STATS (NULL, NULL);
- **Schema** - DBMS_STATS.PUBLISH_PENDING_STATS (schema_name, NULL);
- **Table** - DBMS_STATS.PUBLISH_PENDING_STATS (schema_name, table_name);

GRANULARITY AND INCREMENTAL parameters

For partitioned tables and indexes, DBMS_STATS can gather separate statistics for each partition and global statistics for the entire table or index. The type of partitioning statistics to be gathered is specified in the GRANULARITY argument of the DBMS_STATS gathering procedures. Both types can be important for creating good plans. Oracle recommends setting the GRANULARITY parameter to AUTO to gather both types of partition statistics.

With partitioned tables, new data is often loaded into a new partition. As new partitions are added and data loaded, statistics must be gathered on the new partition, and global statistics must be kept up to date for the entire table. If the INCREMENTAL value for a partition table is set to TRUE, and you gather statistics on that table with the GRANULARITY parameter set to AUTO, Oracle will gather statistics on the new partition and update the global table statistics by scanning only those partitions that have been modified rather than the entire table. If the INCREMENTAL value for the partitioned table is set to FALSE (the default value), then a full table scan is used to maintain the global statistics. This is a highly resource intensive and time consuming operation for large tables. Setting INCREMENTAL to TRUE for a partitioned table requires the SYSAUX tablespace to consume additional space to maintain the global statistics.

New sampling technique

Gathering statistics for a large table can be very time-consuming if the operation reads every row. Sampling a small percentage of the rows provides a much faster operation, albeit with less reliable metrics. The sample size is specified using the ESTIMATE_PERCENT argument of the DBMS_STATS procedures. Prior to 11G, this value has been set to a static value, commonly 5, 10, or 15%. With 11G, Oracle recommends setting the parameter to the new function DBMS_STATS.AUTO_SAMPLE_SIZE. This new function is designed to maximize performance gains while achieving necessary statistical accuracy. AUTO_SAMPLE_SIZE lets Oracle determine the best sample size necessary for good statistics, based on the statistical properties of the particular object.

Multi-Column Statistics

When multiple columns from a single table are used together in the where clause of a query, the relationship between the columns can strongly affect the combined selectivity for the column group. For example, consider a table that has city and state columns. Selecting city and state together produces a much smaller cardinality result than selecting state alone. In 11G, it is possible to create extended statistics against two or more columns. The resulting metrics can be used by the optimizer to provide better access plans when both columns appear in a query.

```
BEGIN
  cg_name := dbms_stats.create_extended_stats
(null,'customer_data',
  '(cust_state,cust_city)');
END;
/
```

```
SELECT sys.dbms_stats.show_extended_stats_name
('sh','customer_data',
       '(cust_state,cust_city)') col_group_name
FROM   dual;
```

You will obtain an output similar to the following:

```
COL_GROUP_NAME
------------------------------
SYS_STU#S#WF25Z#QAHIHE#MOFFMM
```

Expression Statistics

When a function is applied to a column in the where clause of a query (function(col1)=constant), the optimizer has no way of knowing how that function will affect the selectivity of the column. By gathering expression statistics on the expression function(col1), the optimizer will have a more accurate selectivity value. You can also use the create_extended_statistics function to accomplish this:

```
SELECT dbms_stats.create_extended_stats (null,
                                          'customer_data',
                                          '(lower(cust_city))')
FROM   dual;
```

Space Management and Partitioning

Reduce space related error conditions through proactively managing tablespace usage

Oracle assists in proactively managing disk space for tablespaces by creating alerts when available space runs low. Two alert thresholds are defined by default and the database issues alerts for each:

- **Warning** -- The limit at which space is beginning to run low.
- **Critical** -- Is a serious limit that warrants immediate attention.

There are two ways to specify alert thresholds for both locally managed and dictionary managed tablespaces:

- **Percent full** -- When space used becomes greater than or equal to a percent of total space, an alert is issued.
- **Free space remaining** -- When remaining space falls below an amount in KB, an alert is issued.

New locally managed tablespaces are assigned the default threshold values defined for the database. A newly created database has a default of 85% full for the warning threshold and 97% full for the critical threshold. Defaults for free space remaining thresholds for a new database are both zero (disabled). When a new dictionary managed tablespace is created, it is assigned the threshold values that Enterprise Manager lists for "All others" in the metrics categories "Tablespace Free Space (MB) (dictionary managed)" and "Tablespace Space Used (%) (dictionary managed)." For each tablespace, you can set just percent-full thresholds, just free-space-remaining thresholds, or both types of thresholds simultaneously. Setting either type of threshold to zero disables it.

Reclaim wasted space from tables and indexes using the segment shrink functionality

The online segment shrink capability of Oracle allows you to reclaim fragmented free space below the high watermark in a segment. Shrinking a segment provides the following benefits:

- Compaction of data leads to better cache utilization.
- Compacted data requires fewer blocks to be scanned in full table scans.

Segment shrink is an online, in-place operation that does not interfere with DML operations or queries. Concurrent DML operations are blocked for a short time at the end of the shrink operation, when the space is deallocated. Indexes are maintained during the shrink operation and remain usable after completion. No extra disk space needs to be allocated. Segment shrink reclaims unused space both above and below the high water mark. By default, a shrink operation compacts the segment, adjusts the high water mark, and releases the reclaimed space.

Segment shrink requires that rows be moved to new locations. You must first enable row movement in the object and disable any rowid-based triggers. Shrink operations can be performed only on segments in locally managed tablespaces with automatic segment space management (ASSM). Within an ASSM tablespace, all segment types are eligible for online segment shrink except the following:

- IOT mapping tables
- Tables with rowid based materialized views
- Tables with function-based indexes
- SECUREFILE LOBs
- Compressed tables

Invoking Online Segment Shrink

You can shrink space in a table, index-organized table, index, partition, subpartition, materialized view, or materialized view log. You do this using ALTER TABLE, ALTER INDEX, ALTER MATERIALIZED VIEW, or ALTER MATERIALIZED VIEW LOG statement with the SHRINK SPACE clause. There are two optional clauses that control the behavior of the shrink operation:

- **COMPACT** – This clause divides the shrink segment operation into two phases. When specified, the Database defragments the segment space and compacts the table rows but does not reset the high water mark or deallocate space. You can reissue the SHRINK SPACE clause without the COMPACT clause during off-peak hours to complete the shrink operation.
- **CASCADE** – This clause extends the segment shrink operation to all dependent segments of the object.

Examples

Shrink a table and all of its dependent segments:

```
ALTER TABLE employees SHRINK SPACE CASCADE;
```

Shrink a single partition of a partitioned table:

```
ALTER TABLE customers MODIFY PARTITION cust_P1 SHRINK SPACE;
```

Use the Segment Advisor

The Segment Advisor identifies segments that have space available for reclamation. It makes use of AWR data and by sampling data in the segment to generate recommendations. By default it runs during maintenance windows as an automated maintenance task, and can also be run on demand. When run as an automated task, it is called the Automatic Segment Advisor. Segment Advisor generates the following types of advice:

- When an object has a significant amount of free space, it recommends online segment shrink or online table redefinition to reclaim the space.
- When a table could benefit from compression with the OLTP compression method, it makes a recommendation to that effect.
- When a table has row chaining above a certain threshold, it records that fact that the table has an excess of chained rows.

Automatic Segment Advisor

The Automatic Segment Advisor does not analyze every database object. Using AWR data it selects the following objects to analyze:

- Tablespaces that have exceeded a critical or warning space threshold
- Segments that have the most activity
- Segments that have the highest growth rate
- Tables that are at least 10MB and that have at least three indexes to determine the amount of space saved if the tables are compressed with the OLTP compression method.

Viewing Segment Advisor Results

The Segment Advisor creates several types of results: recommendations, findings, actions, and objects. There are several ways to view the results:

- Oracle Enterprise Manager
- Query the DBA_ADVISOR_* views
- Execute the DBMS_SPACE.ASA_RECOMMENDATIONS procedure

Views containing Segment Advisor Data

- **DBA_ADVISOR_RECOMMENDATIONS** -- If a segment would benefit from a segment shrink, reorganization, or compression, the Segment Advisor generates a recommendation for the segment.
- **DBA_ADVISOR_FINDINGS** -- Findings are a report of what the Segment Advisor observed in analyzed segments. Findings include space used and free space statistics for each analyzed segment. Not all findings result in a recommendation.
- **DBA_ADVISOR_ACTIONS** -- Every recommendation is associated with a suggested action to perform: segment shrink, online redefinition (reorganization), or compression. The DBA_ADVISOR_ACTIONS view provides either the SQL that you can use to perform a segment shrink or table compression, or a suggestion to reorganize the object.
- **DBA_ADVISOR_OBJECTS** -- All findings, recommendations, and actions are associated with an object. If the Segment Advisor

analyzes multiple segments, as with a tablespace or partitioned table, then one entry is created in the DBA_ADVISOR_OBJECTS view for each analyzed segment. You can correlate the objects in this view with the objects in the findings, recommendations, and actions views.

Use the Undo Advisor

Automatic tuning of undo retention generally achieves better results with a fixed-size undo tablespace. The Undo Advisor can help you estimate needed capacity for a fixed-side undo tablespace. Undo Advisor can be run via Enterprise Manager or through the DBMS_ADVISOR package. The Undo Advisor uses AWR data for its analysis. AWR must have sufficient workload statistics available for Undo Advisor to make accurate recommendations.

To use the Undo Advisor, you first estimate these two values:

- The length of your expected longest running query
- The longest interval that you will require for Oracle Flashback operations

The maximum of these two values is used as the input to Undo Advisor. The Undo Advisor does not itself alter the size of the undo tablespace. It just returns a recommended size. You must use ALTER DATABASE statements to change a tablespace datafile size.

Undo Advisor is activated by creating an undo advisor task through the advisor framework. The following example creates an undo advisor task to evaluate the undo tablespace. The name of the advisor is 'Undo Advisor'. The analysis is based on Automatic Workload Repository snapshots, which you must specify by setting parameters START_SNAPSHOT and END_SNAPSHOT. In the following example, the START_SNAPSHOT is "1" and END_SNAPSHOT is "100".

```
DECLARE
  tid    NUMBER;
  tname  VARCHAR2(30);
  oid    NUMBER;
BEGIN
  DBMS_ADVISOR.CREATE_TASK('Undo Advisor', tid, tname,
                          'Undo Advisor Task');
  DBMS_ADVISOR.CREATE_OBJECT(tname, 'UNDO_TBS', null, null,
                            null, 'null', oid);
  DBMS_ADVISOR.SET_TASK_PARAMETER(tname, 'TARGET_OBJECTS', oid);
  DBMS_ADVISOR.SET_TASK_PARAMETER(tname, 'START_SNAPSHOT', 1);
  DBMS_ADVISOR.SET_TASK_PARAMETER(tname, 'END_SNAPSHOT', 100);
  DBMS_ADVISOR.SET_TASK_PARAMETER(tname, 'INSTANCE', 1);
  DBMS_ADVISOR.execute_task(tname);
END;
/
```

After you have created the advisor task, you can view the output and recommendations in the Automatic Database Diagnostic Monitor in Enterprise Manager. The information is also available in the DBA_ADVISOR_* data dictionary views

Use Automatic Undo Retention Tuning

Once a transaction has been committed, the undo data is no longer required for rollback or transaction recovery purposes. The data is still necessary for consistent read purposes, however. Long-running queries may require old undo information for producing older images of data blocks. In addition, several Oracle Flashback features make use of old undo information. It is therefore desirable to retain the old undo information for as long as possible.

When the database is using automatic undo management, there is a current undo retention period. This is the minimum amount of time that Oracle Database attempts to retain old undo information before overwriting it. Committed undo information older than the retention period is considered expired and a candidate to be overwritten by new transactions. Old undo information that is less than the retention period is unexpired. Oracle will try not to overwrite unexpired undo, but by default it will so do if failing to overwrite it will cause transactions consuming undo to fail.

The undo retention period is automatically tuned based on undo tablespace size and system activity. You can optionally specify a minimum undo retention period (in seconds) by setting the UNDO_RETENTION initialization parameter. Setting this parameter has the following impact:

- **Fixed-Size Undo tablespace** -- The parameter is ignored. The database always tunes the undo retention period for the best possible retention, based on system activity and undo tablespace size.
- **Undo tablespace with AUTOEXTEND** -- If space is low and the value of UNDO_RETENTION has not been met, instead of overwriting unexpired undo information, the tablespace auto-extends. If the tablespace has a MAXSIZE, when the maximum size is reached, the database will begin to overwrite unexpired undo information.

Implement the new partitioning methods

Interval Partitioning

Range partitioning maps data to partitions using ranges of key values that you establish for each partition. Interval partitioning is an extension of this concept. With interval partitioning, you instruct the database to automatically create partitions of a specified interval when inserted data exceeds the range partitions. The table must have at least one range partition. The range partitioning key value determines the high value of the range partitions -- called the transition point. The database will create interval partitions for data beyond that point.

Interval partitioning has the following restrictions:

- You can only specify one partitioning key column, and it must be of NUMBER or DATE type.
- Interval partitioning is not supported for index-organized tables.
- You cannot create a domain index on an interval-partitioned table.

Reference Partitioning

Reference partitioning is used with two tables that are related to one another by referential constraints. The partitioning key is inherited through an existing parent-child relationship, and it is enforced by enabled and active primary key and foreign key constraints. With this partitioning method, dependent tables with a child relationship can be logically equi-partitioned by inheriting the partitioning key from the parent table. The reference dependency will automatically cascade partition maintenance operations. For example, take a parent table of Orders, with a child table of order items with an enforced foreign key relationship. If Orders were to be partitioned by year, using the "Order Date" column, the OrderItems table could be reference partitioned and would be partitioned by the 'Order Date' column even though that column is not part of the OrderItems table.

System Partitioning

System partitioning is different from every other partitioning method in that there is no partition key. System partitioning is application-controlled partitioning where the Oracle database is not controlling the data placement. The database allows the application to break a table into partitions without knowing what the individual partitions are for. All partitioning functions are controlled entirely by the application. Inserting a row into a system partitioned table without explicitly specifying a partition will fail. System partitioning does not provide performance enhancements as partition pruning and partition-wise joins are not possible with it.

Partitioning on Virtual Columns

Prior to 11G, a table could only be partitioned if the partitioning key physically existed in the table. In 11G it's possible for a partitioning key to be defined by an expression using one or more existing columns of a table. Virtual column-based Partitioning is supported with all basic partitioning strategies, including interval and composite partitioning.

Additional Composite Partitioning

Composite partitioning is a combination of two partitioning operations. A table is partitioned by one data distribution method and then each partition is further subdivided into subpartitions using a second logic. The subpartitions for a given partition represent a logical subset of the data. The two operations might be the same partition style (i.e. both Range), or different styles. The valid combinations of composite partitioning in 11G are:

- Range-Range; Range-Hash; Range-List
- List-Range; List-Hash; List-List
- Interval-Range; Interval-Hash; Interval-List

Employ Data Compression

Enhanced Table Compression

Table compression saves disk space and reduces memory use in the buffer cache. It can also speed up query execution during reads at the expense of incurring additional CPU overhead. Table compression is specified using the COMPRESS clause of the CREATE TABLE and ALTER TABLE statements. If compression is added to a table via ALTER TABLE, only data inserted or updated after the ALTER operation will be compressed. You can disable table compression with ALTER TABLE...NOCOMPRESS. In this case, all data that was already compressed remains compressed, and new data is inserted uncompressed. Table compression is transparent to applications.

You can enable compression for all table operations or you can enable it for direct-path inserts only. COMPATIBLE must be set to 11.1 or higher in order to enable compression for conventional DML. To enable compression for all operations you must use the COMPRESS FOR ALL OPERATIONS clause. To enable compression for direct-path inserts only, you use the COMPRESS FOR DIRECT_LOAD OPERATIONS clause. The keyword COMPRESS by itself is equivalent to the clause COMPRESS FOR DIRECT_LOAD OPERATIONS that existed in Oracle 10G.

New RMAN Compression: ZLIB

Prior to 11g Oracle RMAN used a single compression algorithm, called BZIP2. The algorithm performed very well in terms of the compression ratio in decreasing the size of RMAN files. However, it has a high CPU cost which makes it unsuitable for sites having CPU bottlenecks. With 11g, Oracle introduced a new compression algorithm, ZLIB. ZLIB is 40-50% faster than BZIP2 and has a compression ratio of about 1.68:1 to BZIP's 2:1. ZLIB is the default compression algorithm for RMAN in 11G. You can change this using the command:

```
RMAN> configure compression algorithm 'bzip2';
```

SecureFiles Compression

SecureFiles was discussed in more detail in a prior chapter. It's worth noting here that SecureFiles has a built in capability for compression that is separate from the two just discussed.

Load and Unload Data

Transport tablespaces across different platforms

The Transportable Tablespaces feature enables you to copy a tablespace from one Oracle Database to another. The tablespace can be locally or dictionary managed and is does not have to be the same block size as the destination database standard block size. Moving data using transportable tablespaces is much faster than either an export/import or unload/load of the same data. This is because the datafiles are copied to the destination location, and Data Pump is used just to transfer the metadata for the objects it contains to the new database.

There are two ways to transport a tablespace:

- Issuing manual commands via SQL*Plus, RMAN, and Data Pump.
- Using the Transport Tablespaces Wizard in Enterprise Manager

It is possible to transport tablespaces across platforms. Not all platforms are supported for cross-platform transport. You can determine if an OS is supported by querying the V$TRANSPORTABLE_PLATFORM view. This view also indicates each platform's endian format (byte ordering). If the source and destination platforms are of different endianness, then an additional step is required to convert the tablespace being transported. The following query displays the platforms that support cross-platform tablespace transport:

```
SELECT platform_id PID, platform_name, endian_format
FROM   v$transportable_platform
WHERE  platform_name LIKE '%Linux%'
ORDER BY platform_name;

PID  PLATFORM_NAME         ENDIAN_FORMAT
---- --------------------- --------------
10   Linux IA (32-bit)     Little
11   Linux IA (64-bit)     Little
13   Linux x86 64-bit      Little
```

Before a tablespace can be transported to a different platform, the datafile header must identify the platform to which it belongs. In an

Oracle Database with compatibility set to 10.0.0 or later, you can accomplish this by making the datafile read/write at least once.

The following limitations apply to transporting tablespaces:

- The source and the destination databases must use compatible database character sets.
- The destination database cannot contain a tablespace of the same name. If it does, you must rename either the tablespace to be transported or the one in the destination database.
- Objects with underlying objects (such as materialized views) or contained objects (such as partitioned tables) are not transportable unless all of the underlying or contained objects are in the tablespace being transported.
- Encrypted tablespaces have several conditions (See the Admin Guide for more details).
- Tablespaces that do not use block encryption but that contain tables with encrypted columns cannot be transported.

Steps to Transport a Tablespace

Task 1: Determine if Platforms are Supported and Determine Endianness

This task is only required if the source and destination platforms are different. If both platforms are supported, you can perform the transport. However, if they do not have the same endianness, you must perform a conversion of the tablespace set either at the source or destination database. To determine of the platforms are supported and their endianness, query the V$TRANSPORTABLE_PLATFORM view.

Task 2: Pick a Self-Contained Set of Tablespaces

It is only possible to transport a set of tablespaces that has no references from inside the set of tablespaces pointing outside of the tablespaces. An example of a violation to this rule would be an index inside the set of tablespaces that is for a table outside of the set. You can call the TRANSPORT_SET_CHECK procedure in the package DBMS_TTS to check if a tablespace is self-contained. The following statement can be used to determine whether tablespace ocpts is self-contained, with referential integrity constraints taken into consideration (indicated by TRUE).

```
EXECUTE DBMS_TTS.TRANSPORT_SET_CHECK('ocpts', TRUE);
```

Any violations will be visible in the TRANSPORT_SET_VIOLATIONS view. If the set of tablespaces is self-contained, this view is empty. Violations must be resolved before the tablespace can be transported.

Task 3: Generate a Transportable Tablespace Set

1. Start SQL*Plus and connect to the database as an administrator or as a user who has either the ALTER TABLESPACE or MANAGE TABLESPACE system privilege.
2. Make all tablespaces in the set read-only.
3. Invoke the Data Pump export utility as user system and specify the tablespaces in the transportable set.
4. Check the log file for errors
5. When finished, exit back to SQL*Plus:

If the tablespace is being transported to a platform with a different endianness, you can convert it before transporting the tablespace set. To convert the datafiles, you will use the RMAN CONVERT TABLESPACE command.

Task 4: Transport the Tablespace Set

Complete the following steps:

1. Transport both the datafiles and the export (dump) file of the tablespaces the destination database.

2. If you are transporting the tablespace set to a platform with a different endianness than the source platform, and have not yet converted the tablespace set, do so now with the RMAN CONVERT TABLESPACE command.

Task 5: (Optional) Restore Tablespaces to Read/Write Mode

Make the transported tablespaces read/write again at the source database.

Task 6: Import the Tablespace Set

Any privileged user can perform this task. To import a tablespace set, complete the following steps:

1. Import the tablespace metadata using the Data Pump Import utility, impdp:
2. If required, put the tablespaces into read/write mode on the destination database.

Explain Data Pump architecture

Oracle Data Pump is made up of three distinct parts:

- **expdp and impdp** -- These are command-line clients that use the procedures provided in the DBMS_DATAPUMP package to execute export and import commands. They accept parameters entered at the command line that enable the exporting and importing of data and metadata for a complete database or for subsets of a database.
- **DBMS_DATAPUMP** -- Also known as the Data Pump API, this package provides a high-speed mechanism to move all or part of the data and metadata for a site from one database to another. DBMS_DATAPUMP can be used independently of the impdp and expdp clients.

- **DBMS_METADATA** -- Also known as the Metadata API, this package provides a centralized facility for the extraction, manipulation, and re-creation of dictionary metadata. DBMS_METADATA can be used independently of the impdp and expdp clients.

Data Pump jobs use a master table, a master process, and worker processes to perform the work and keep track of progress:

- **Master Table** -- A master table is used to track the progress within a job while the data and metadata are being transferred. It is implemented as a user table within the database. A user performing an impdp or expdp must have the CREATE TABLE system privilege for the master table to be created plus sufficient tablespace quota. The master table will have the same name as the job that created it. A Data Pump job cannot have the same name as an existing table or view in that schema. The information in the master table is used to restart a job.
- **Master process** -- A master process is created for every Data Pump Export job and Data Pump Import job. It controls the entire job, including communicating with the clients, creating and controlling a pool of worker processes, and performing logging operations.
- **Worker Process** -- The master process allocates work to be executed to worker processes that perform the data and metadata processing within an operation. Data Pump can employ multiple worker processes, running in parallel, to increase job performance.

Monitor a Data Pump job

It's possible to use the Data Pump Export and Import utilities to attach to a running job. When attached in logging mode, status about the job is automatically displayed during execution in real-time. When attached using interactive-command mode, it's possible to request the job status.

Optionally, a log file can be written during the execution of a job. It summarizes the progress of the job, lists any errors, and records the completion status. You can also determine job status or to get other information about Data Pump jobs, through the data pump views:

- **DBA_DATAPUMP_JOBS** -- Identifies all active Data Pump jobs in the database, regardless of their state, on an instance (or on all instances for RAC). It also shows all Data Pump master tables not currently associated with an active job.
- **DBA_DATAPUMP_SESSIONS** -- Identifies the user sessions that are attached to a Data Pump job. The information in this view is useful for determining why a stopped Data Pump operation has not gone away.
- **V$SESSION_LONGOPS** -- Data Pump operations that transfer table data (export and import) maintain an entry indicating the job progress. The entry contains the estimated transfer size and is periodically updated to reflect the actual amount of data transferred.

The V$SESSION_LONGOPS columns that are relevant to a Data Pump job are as follows:

- **USERNAME** - job owner
- **OPNAME** - job name
- **TARGET_DESC** - job operation
- **SOFAR** - megabytes transferred thus far during the job
- **TOTALWORK** - estimated number of megabytes in the job
- **UNITS** - megabytes (MB)
- **MESSAGE** - a formatted status message of the form: 'job_name: operation_name : nnn out of mmm MB done'

Use Data Pump export and import

The Data Pump Export utility is invoked using the expdp command. The actions performed by the export operation are defined by the parameters you specify. They can be supplied either on the command line or in a parameter file. Data Pump Export can be controlled using a command line, a parameter file, or an interactive-command mode.

- **Command-Line** -- Enables you to specify most of the export parameters from the command line.
- **Parameter File** -- Allows you to specify command-line parameters in a parameter file. The PARFILE parameter cannot be used in a parameter file, because parameter files cannot be nested.
- **Interactive-Command** -- Displays an export prompt from which you can enter various commands. Some commands are specific to interactive-command mode.

Data Pump jobs manage the following types of files:

- **Dump files** -- Contain the data and metadata being moved.
- **Log files** -- Record the messages associated with an operation.
- **SQL files** -- Record the output of a SQLFILE operation.
- **Data Files** -- Files specified by the DATA_FILES parameter during a transportable import.

There are different expdp modes for unloading different portions of the database. The mode is specified using the appropriate parameter. The available modes are:

- **Full Export** -- In a full database export, the entire database is unloaded. This mode requires the user performing the export to have the DATAPUMP_EXP_FULL_DATABASE role. Specified using the FULL parameter.
- **Schema** -- This is the default export mode. If you have the DATAPUMP_EXP_FULL_DATABASE role, then you can provide a list of schemas to export. Otherwise you can export only your own schema. Specified using the SCHEMAS parameter.
- **Table** -- In table mode, only a specified set of tables, partitions, and their dependent objects are unloaded. You must have the DATAPUMP_EXP_FULL_DATABASE role to export tables that are not in your own schema. Specified using the TABLES parameter.
- **Tablespace** -- In tablespace mode, only the tables contained in a specified set of tablespaces are unloaded. If a table is unloaded, then its dependent objects are also unloaded. Privileged users get

all tables. Unprivileged users get only the tables in their own schemas. Specified using the TABLESPACES parameter.

- **Transportable Tablespace** -- In transportable tablespace mode, only the metadata for the tables (and their dependent objects) within a specified set of tablespaces is exported. The tablespace data files are copied in a separate operation. Specified using the TRANSPORT_TABLESPACES parameter.

expdp Parameters

The following parameters are applicable to expdp:

- **ATTACH** -- Attaches the client session to an existing export job and automatically places you in the interactive-command interface.
- **CONTENT** -- Enables you to filter what Export unloads: data only, metadata only, or both.
- **DIRECTORY** -- Specifies the default location to which Export can write the dump file set and the log file.
- **DUMPFILE** -- Specifies the names, and optionally, the directory objects of dump files for an export job.
- **ESTIMATE** -- Specifies the method that Export will use to estimate how much disk space each table in the export job will consume (in bytes).
- **ESTIMATE_ONLY** -- Instructs Export to estimate the space that a job would consume, without actually performing the export operation.
- **EXCLUDE** -- Enables you to filter the metadata that is exported by specifying objects and object types to be excluded from the export operation.
- **FILESIZE** -- Specifies the maximum size of each dump file.
- **FLASHBACK_SCN** -- Specifies the system change number (SCN) that Export will use to enable the Flashback Query utility.
- **FLASHBACK_TIME** -- The SCN that most closely matches the specified time is found, and this SCN is used to enable the Flashback utility.
- **FULL** -- Specifies that you want to perform a full database mode export.

- **INCLUDE** -- Enables you to filter the metadata that is exported by specifying objects and object types for the current export mode.
- **JOB_NAME** -- Used to identify the export job in subsequent actions.
- **KEEP_MASTER** -- Indicates whether the master table should be deleted or retained at the end of a Data Pump job that completes successfully.
- **LOGFILE** -- Specifies the name, and optionally, a directory, for the log file of the export job.
- **PARALLEL** -- Specifies the maximum number of processes of active execution operating on behalf of the export job.
- **PARFILE** -- Specifies the name of an export parameter file.
- **QUERY** -- Allows you to specify a query clause that is used to filter the data that gets exported.
- **SCHEMAS** -- Specifies that you want to perform a schema-mode export.
- **TABLES** -- Specifies that you want to perform a table-mode export.
- **TABLESPACES** -- Specifies a list of tablespace names to be exported in tablespace mode.
- **TRANSPORT_FULL_CHECK** -- Specifies whether to check for dependencies between those objects inside the transportable set and those outside the transportable set.
- **TRANSPORT_TABLESPACES** -- Specifies that you want to perform an export in transportable-tablespace mode.

impdp Parameters

Many of the above parameters are also applicable to impdp. In addition, several of the more common impdp parameters are:

- **REUSE_DATAFILES** -- Specifies whether the import job should reuse existing data files for tablespace creation.
- **SKIP_UNUSABLE_INDEXES** -- Specifies whether Import skips loading tables that have indexes that were set to the Index Unusable state
- **SQLFILE** -- Specifies a file into which all of the SQL DDL that Import would have executed, based on other parameters, is written.

- **STATUS** -- Specifies the frequency at which the job status display is updated.
- **TABLE_EXISTS_ACTION** -- Tells Import what to do if the table it is trying to create already exists.
- **TRANSPORT_DATAFILES** -- Specifies a list of data files to be imported into the target database by a transportable-tablespace mode import, or by a table-mode import if TRANSPORTABLE=ALWAYS was set during the export.
- **REMAP_DATAFILE** -- Changes the name of the source data file to the target data file name in all SQL statements where the source data file is referenced.
- **REMAP_SCHEMA** -- Loads all objects from the source schema into a target schema.
- **REMAP_TABLE** -- Allows you to rename tables during an import operation.
- **REMAP_TABLESPACE** -- Remaps all objects selected for import with persistent data in the source tablespace to be created in the target tablespace.
- **TRANSFORM** -- Enables you to alter object creation DDL for objects being imported.

The following commands are applicable when using Interactive mode:

- **ADD_FILE** -- Add additional dump files.
- **CONTINUE_CLIENT** -- Exit interactive mode and enter logging mode.
- **EXIT_CLIENT** -- Stop the export client session, but leave the job running.
- **KILL_JOB** -- Detach all currently attached client sessions and terminate the current job.
- **PARALLEL** -- Increase or decrease the number of active worker processes for the current job.
- **START_JOB** -- Restart a stopped job to which you are attached.
- **STATUS** -- Display detailed status for the current job and/or set status interval.
- **STOP_JOB** -- Stop the current job for later restart.

Create external tables for data population

External tables are defined as tables that do not reside in the database. It's possible to have tables in any format for which an access driver is provided. Inside the Oracle data dictionary is stored metadata describing an external table. With this metadata, Oracle provides SQL access to the external table as if it were a regular database table. It's possible to perform SELECT and JOIN operations, or create views of synonyms against external tables. it is not possible to perform DML operations or create indexes on external tables.

The metadata for external tables is created using the ORGANIZATION EXTERNAL clause of the CREATE TABLEL statement. An external table definition acts as a view against the external data. An access driver is mechanism by which the external data is read. Oracle Database provides two access drivers for external tables: ORACLE_LOADER and ORACLE_DATAPUMP. ORACLE_LOADER reads data from external files using the Oracle loader technology using a subset of the control file syntax of the SQL*Loader utility. ORACLE_DATAPUMP, allows you to read data from the database and insert it into an external table, and then reload it into an Oracle Database. Note that while ORACLE_LOADER allows writing to external files, the functionality is not performed via DML statements. The ANALYZE statement is not supported for gathering statistics for external tables, but you can use the DBMS_STATS package. Virtual columns are not supported on external tables. For an external table, the DROP TABLE statement removes only metadata in the database. It has no affect on the actual data outside of the database.

You create external tables using the CREATE TABLE statement with an ORGANIZATION EXTERNAL clause. This statement creates only metadata in the data dictionary. The following example creates an external table using the ORACLE_LOADER access method.

```
CREATE TABLE phone_list_ext (
  employee_id        VARCHAR2(5),
  first_name         VARCHAR2(50),
  last_name          VARCHAR2(50),
  phone              VARCHAR2(20)
)
ORGANIZATION EXTERNAL (
  TYPE ORACLE_LOADER
  DEFAULT DIRECTORY ext_tables
  ACCESS PARAMETERS (
    RECORDS DELIMITED BY NEWLINE
    FIELDS TERMINATED BY ','
    MISSING FIELD VALUES ARE NULL
    (
      employee_id        CHAR(5),
      first_name         CHAR(50),
      last_name          CHAR(50),
      phone              CHAR(20)
    )
  )
  LOCATION ('phone_list.txt')
)
PARALLEL 2
REJECT LIMIT UNLIMITED;
```

The example above uses the ORACLE_LOADER access driver. This driver is used for reading text files. Essentially any file that SQL*Loader can read from can be used as an external table. The parameters in the ACCESS PARAMETERS clause are opaque to the database. These access parameters are specific to the access driver. Oracle provides these parameters to the access driver when the external table is accessed. The PARALLEL clause enables parallel query on the data sources. The REJECT LIMIT clause specifies that there is no limit on the number of errors that can occur during a query of the external data.

Only the following ALTER TABLE Clause options are allowed on external tables:

- **REJECT LIMIT** -- Changes the reject limit
- **PROJECT COLUMN REFERENCED** -- The access driver processes only the columns in the select list of the query. This setting may

not provide a consistent set of rows when querying a different column list from the same external table but can speed up access.

- **PROJECT COLUMN ALL** -- the access driver processes all of the columns defined on the external table. This setting always provides a consistent set of rows when querying an external table. This is the default.
- **DEFAULT DIRECTORY** -- Changes the default directory specification

Backup and Recovery Enhancements

Simplify file management for all recovery-related files

The Fast Recovery Area is a location in which the database can store and manage files related to backup and recovery. The location is separate from the database area, where the current database files are located. The fast recovery area can contain control files, online redo logs, archived redo logs, flashback logs, and RMAN backups. Files in the recovery area are labeled as permanent or transient. Permanent files are active files used by the database instance -- all others are transient. Transient files are generally deleted after they become obsolete or have been backed up to tape. The fast recovery area is location that can be used to hold RMAN disk backups, control file autobackups and archived redo log files. Files placed in this location are maintained by Oracle Database and the generated file names are maintained in Oracle Managed Files (OMF) format.

You must specify the following initialization parameters to enable the Fast Recovery Area:

- **DB_RECOVERY_FILE_DEST** -- Location of the Fast Recovery Area. This can be a directory, file system, or Automatic Storage Management (Oracle ASM) disk group. It cannot be a raw file system.
- **DB_RECOVERY_FILE_DEST_SIZE** -- Specifies the maximum total bytes to be used by the Fast Recovery Area. This initialization parameter must be specified before DB_RECOVERY_FILE_DEST is enabled.

These parameters cannot be enabled if you have set values for the parameters LOG_ARCHIVE_DEST and LOG_ARCHIVE_DUPLEX_DEST. You must disable those parameters before setting up the Fast Recovery Area. You can instead set values for the LOG_ARCHIVE_DEST_n parameters. The

LOG_ARCHIVE_DEST_1 parameter is implicitly set to point to the Fast Recovery Area if a local archiving location has not been configured and LOG_ARCHIVE_DEST_1 value has not been set.

Managing Space in the Fast Recovery Area

The database issues a warning alert when reclaimable space is less than 15% and a critical alert when reclaimable space is less than 3%. An entry is added to the alert log and to the DBA_OUTSTANDING_ALERTS table to warn the DBA of this condition. If not resolved, the database will consume space in the fast recovery area until there is no space left.

You can resolve low space issues in the Fast Recovery Area in several ways:

- Make more disk space available and increase DB_RECOVERY_FILE_DEST_SIZE.
- Move backups from the fast recovery area to tertiary storage such as tape. The BACKUP RECOVERY AREA command will back up all of your recovery area files to tape.
- Run DELETE for any files that have been removed with an operating system utility. The database is not aware of file removed by OS commands.
- Run the RMAN CROSSCHECK command to have RMAN recheck the contents of the fast recovery area and identify expired files, and then use the DELETE EXPIRED command to delete every expired backup from the RMAN repository.
- Delete any unnecessary guaranteed restore points.
- Review your backup retention policy and make it less restrictive.

Information about the Fast Recovery Area is stored in the V$RECOVERY_FILE_DEST dynamic view. In addition, the column IS_RECOVERY_DET_FILE has been added to the following views: V$CONTROLFILE, V$LOGFILE, V$ARCHIVED_LOG, V$DATAFILE_COPY, V$DATAFILE, V$BACKUP_PIECE and the RMAN tables. This column has a value of YES if a file of the corresponding kind has been created in the fast recovery area.

Reduce restore time by applying incremental backups to data file image copies

The RMAN BACKUP INCREMENTAL command creates an incremental backup of a database. Incremental backups capture block-level changes to a database made after a previous incremental backup. Recovery with incremental backups is faster than using redo logs alone. There are three types of incremental backups:

- **Level 0** -- This is the starting point for an incremental backup. It backs up all blocks in the database and is identical in content to a full backup.
- **Level 1 Differential** -- This backup contains only blocks changed since the most recent incremental backup. This is the default Level 1 backup.
- **Level 1 Cumulative** -- This backup contains only blocks changed since the most recent level 0 backup.

When restoring incremental backups, RMAN uses the level 0 backup as the starting point. It then uses the level 1 backups to updates changed blocks where possible to avoid reapplying changes from redo one at a time. If incremental backups are available, then RMAN uses them during recovery.

The following example creates a level 0 incremental backup to serve as a base for an incremental backup strategy:

```
BACKUP INCREMENTAL LEVEL 0 DATABASE;
```

The following example creates a level 1 cumulative incremental backup:

```
BACKUP INCREMENTAL LEVEL 1 CUMULATIVE DATABASE;
```

The following example creates a level 1 differential incremental backup:

```
BACKUP INCREMENTAL LEVEL 1 DATABASE;
```

The RMAN incrementally updated backup strategy has the following main features:

- A level 0 data file copy is created as a base. This copy has either a system-defined or user-defined tag.
- Periodically, level 1 differential backups are created with the same tag as the level 0 data file copy.
- Periodically, the incremental backups are applied to the level 0 data file copy. Because the data file copy has been updated with more recent changes, it now requires less media recovery.

Simplify recovery after opening the database with the RESETLOGS option

When you open the database with the RESETLOGS option, the database performs the following actions:

- Archives the current online redo logs and then erases the contents of the online redo logs and resets the log sequence number to 1.
- Creates the online redo log files if they do not currently exist.
- Initializes redo thread records and online redo log records in the control file to the beginning of the new database incarnation.
- Updates all current datafiles and online redo logs and all subsequent archived redo logs with a new RESETLOGS SCN and time stamp.

Effectively what the above means is that the Oracle is now able to distinguish the difference between archive logs created before the RESETLOGS operation and those after it. This prevents a datafile from being corrupted by applying archived logs that are not from direct parent incarnations of the current incarnation. In previous releases, it was recommended that you back up the database immediately after an OPEN RESETLOGS. The new behavior allows you to recover a pre-RESETLOGS backup like any other backup. To perform recovery through RESETLOGS you must have all archived logs generated after the most recent backup and at least one control file (current, backup, or created)..

Speed backup times by creating faster incremental backups

The block change tracking feature improves backup performance for incremental backups by recording changed blocks for each data file. If block change tracking is enabled, RMAN uses a block change tracking file to identify changed blocks during incremental backups. This file keeps RMAN from having to scan every block in the data file that it is backing up. Block change tracking is disabled by default. One block change tracking file is created for the whole database. By default, the change tracking file is created as an Oracle managed file in the destination specified by the DB_CREATE_FILE_DEST initialization parameter.

To enable block change tracking, execute the following ALTER DATABASE statement:

```
ALTER DATABASE ENABLE BLOCK CHANGE TRACKING;
```

You can also create the change tracking file in a specific location:

```
ALTER DATABASE ENABLE BLOCK CHANGE TRACKING
USING FILE '/ocpdir/rman_change_track.f' REUSE;
```

You can disable block change tracking by executing the following command:

```
ALTER DATABASE DISABLE BLOCK CHANGE TRACKING;
```

The V$BLOCK_CHANGE_TRACKING view can be used to determine whether change tracking is enabled, and the file name of the block change tracking file.

```
SELECT status, filename
FROM   v$block_change_tracking;

STATUS   FILENAME
-------- ---------------------------------------------------
ENABLED  /u01/ocp/RDBMS/changetracking/e1_cs_2e61nr6j_.chg
```

Minimize load requirements by specifying limits in backup time windows

You can use the DURATION parameter of the BACKUP command to limit the amount of time a given backup job is given to run. To specify a backup duration:

```
BACKUP
DURATION 4:00
TABLESPACE users;
```

The above command will generate an error if the backup does not complete inside the window. If the keyword PARTIAL is specified, RMAN does not report an error but rather displays a message showing which files are not backed up. If the BACKUP command is part of a RUN block, then the remaining commands in the RUN block continue to execute. Specifying FILESPERSET of 1 will save each file as its own backup set. If the window closes before the backup is complete, only the current set (one file) is lost. To prevent RMAN from issuing an error and minimize lost work when a backup partially completes:

```
BACKUP
DURATION 4:00 PARTIAL
TABLESPACE users
FILESPERSET 1;
```

Minimizing Backup Load and Duration

When using DURATION you can run the backup with the maximum possible performance, or run as slowly as possible while still finishing within the allotted time, to minimize the performance impact of backup tasks. To maximize performance, use the MINIMIZE TIME option with DURATION.

```
BACKUP
DURATION 4:00 PARTIAL
MINIMIZE TIME
DATABASE
FILESPERSET 1;
```

When MINIMIZE LOAD is specified, RMAN monitors the progress of the running backup, and periodically estimates how long the backup takes to complete at its present rate. If RMAN estimates that the backup will finish before the end of the backup window, then it slows down the rate of backup so that the full available duration is used. This reduces the overhead on the database associated with the backup. To extend the backup to use the full time available, use the MINIMIZE LOAD option:

```
BACKUP
DURATION 4:00 PARTIAL
MINIMIZE LOAD
DATABASE
FILESPERSET 1;
```

Save storage space through writing compressed backup sets

For any use of the BACKUP command that creates backup sets, you can use binary compression of backup sets. Add the AS COMPRESSED BACKUPSET option to the BACKUP command. RMAN will compress the backup set contents before writing to disk. Information regarding the binary compression level used is automatically recorded in the backup set. When recovering, there is no need to explicitly mention the type of compression used or how to decompress. Binary compression imposes a performance overhead during backup and restore operations. It consumes CPU resources, so compressed backups should not be scheduled when CPU usage is high. An example of a command to make a compressed backup is:

```
BACKUP
AS COMPRESSED BACKUPSET
DATABASE PLUS ARCHIVELOG;
```

Managing Archive logs

Oracle 11G simplifies archive log management when used by multiple components. The archivelog deletion policy can be used to ensure the logs are deleted only when they are no longer needed by required components (e.g. Data Guard, Streams, and Flashback). In a Data Guard environment, all standby destinations can be considered where logs are applied, before marking archive logs to be deleted. This configuration is specified using CONFIGURE ARCHIVELOG DELETION POLICY TO APPLIED ON ALL STANDBY.

In addition 11G increases availability when backing up archive logs. It allows an optional archive log destination to be utilized in the event that the flash recovery area is inaccessible during backup. If this happens, the backup will use a copy from the optional destination and continue backing up the archive logs.

Using Flashback and Logminer

Configure and use Flashback Database

Flashback database is useful feature introduced with 10g that allows the database to be essentially moved back in time. The requirements for enabling Flashback Database are:

- The database must be running in ARCHIVELOG mode, because archived logs are used.
- The database must have a flash recovery area enabled.
- For RAC databases, the flash recovery area must be stored in a clustered file system or in ASM.

In order to enable the Flashback Database feature for the whole database, the database must be mounted, but not open.

```
SHUTDOWN IMMEDIATE;
STARTUP MOUNT;
ALTER DATABASE FLASHBACK ON;
```

The DB_FLASHBACK_RETENTION_TARGET initialization parameter defaults to one day of flashback information. If you want more or less, you must alter the parameter value. It is defined in minutes.

```
ALTER SYSTEM SET DB_FLASHBACK_RETENTION_TARGET=4320; # 3 days
```

By default, when flashback logging is enabled, flashback logs will be generated for all permanent tablespaces. You can reduce overhead by disabling flashback logging for specific tablespaces. However, if you disable flashback logs for a tablespace, its datafiles must be taken offline before running FLASHBACK DATABASE.

```
ALTER TABLESPACE ocp_3 FLASHBACK OFF;
```

You can disable flashback logging for the entire database with this command:

```
SQL> ALTER DATABASE FLASHBACK OFF;
```

When using Flashback Database, you must add extra space to the flash recovery area to hold the flashback logs, along with the other files stored in the flash recovery area.

Recover dropped tables with the Flashback Drop feature

By default, when a table is dropped, the database does not immediately remove the space associated with the table. Instead, the database renames it and places the table and any associated objects that were dropped in a recycle bin. If it is determined that the table was dropped in error, it can be recovered at a later date. The FLASHBACK TABLE statement is used to restore the table. The recycle bin is a data dictionary table that contains information required to recover dropped objects. The dropped objects themselves remain where they were before being dropped and still occupy the same amount of disk space. Dropped objects also continue to count against user space quotas until they are explicitly purged or are purged by the database due to tablespace space constraints. When a tablespace including its contents is dropped, the recycle bin does not come into play. The storage where the objects were does not exist. The database purges any entries in the recycle bin for objects that were located in the tablespace. If the recycle bin is disabled, dropped tables and their dependent objects are not placed in the recycle bin; they are just dropped. They must be recovered by other means, such as recovering from backup. The recycle bin is enabled by default.

The FLASHBACK TABLE ... TO BEFORE DROP statement is used to recover objects from the recycle bin. When recovering a table, you must specify either the system-generated name of the table in the recycle bin or the original table name. An optional RENAME TO clause lets you rename the table as you recover it. The USER_RECYCLEBIN view can be used to obtain the system-generated name. To use the FLASHBACK TABLE ... TO BEFORE DROP statement, you need the same privileges required to drop the table.

The following example restores ocp_employees table and assigns to it a new name:

```
FLASHBACK TABLE ocp_employees TO BEFORE DROP
RENAME TO ocp_employees_take2;
```

Retrieve row history information with the Flashback Versions Query feature

Flashback Version Query is used to retrieve metadata and historical data for a specific interval. The interval can be specified by two timestamps or by two SCNs. The metadata returned includes the start and end time a version existed, type of DML operation used to create it, and the identity of the transaction that created each row version. The VERSIONS BETWEEN clause of a SELECT statement is used to generate a Flashback Version Query. The syntax of the VERSIONS BETWEEN clause is: VERSIONS {BETWEEN {SCN | TIMESTAMP} start AND end}.

The Pseudocolumns returned by a Flashback version query are:

- **VERSIONS_START[SCN/TIME]** -- Starting System Change Number (SCN) or TIMESTAMP when the row version was created. NULL if version is from before the start value.
- **VERSIONS_END[SCN/TIME]** -- SCN or TIMESTAMP when the row version expired. If NULL, then either the row version was current at the time of the query or the row is for a DELETE operation.
- **VERSIONS_XID** -- Identifier of the transaction that created the row version.
- **VERSIONS_OPERATION** -- Operation performed by the transaction: I for insertion, D for deletion, or U for update. The version is that of the row that was inserted, deleted, or updated.

A given row version is valid starting at VERSIONS_START* up to, but not including, VERSIONS_END*. That is, it is valid for any time 't' such that VERSIONS_START* <= t < VERSIONS_END*. The following three updates were issued against the EMPLOYEES table, with a pause in-between.

```
UPDATE employees SET salary = 97000
WHERE emp_last='McCoy';
UPDATE employees SET salary = 102000
WHERE emp_last='McCoy';
UPDATE employees SET salary = 105000
WHERE emp_last='McCoy';
COMMIT;
```

Then the following Flashback Versions query was run against employees:

```
SELECT versions_starttime, versions_endtime,
       versions_xid, versions_operation AS OP,
       salary
  FROM employees
  VERSIONS BETWEEN TIMESTAMP
      TO_TIMESTAMP('29-MAR-12 11.46.00PM','DD-MON-YY HH:MI:SSAM')
  AND TO_TIMESTAMP('29-MAR-12 11.52.00PM','DD-MON-YY HH:MI:SSAM')
  WHERE emp_last = 'McCoy';
```

```
VERSIONS_STARTTIME   VERSIONS_ENDTIME      VERSIONS_XID     OP SALARY
-------------------- --------------------- ---------------- -- ------
29-MAR-12 11.51.08PM                       09000900A9010000 U  105000
29-MAR-12 11.49.50PM 29-MAR-12 11.51.08PM 04001A003F010000 U  102000
29-MAR-12 11.49.02PM 29-MAR-12 11.49.50PM 03002100A2010000 U   97000
                     29-MAR-12 11.49.02PM                      93500
```

From the results above, you see the three updates against the table, each increasing the salary column value. It's clear when each salary value started and ended (save the initial value for which the start time was outside the window, and the end value which is current (and therefore has no end time). You can use VERSIONS_XID with Oracle Flashback Transaction Query to locate the metadata for any of the three transactions. This will include the SQL required to undo the row change and the user responsible for the change.

Audit or recover FROM transactions with the Flashback Transaction Query feature

A Flashback Transaction Query is used to retrieve metadata and historical data for a single transaction or for all transactions in a supplied interval. The data is generated from the static data dictionary view FLASHBACK_TRANSACTION_QUERY. The Flashback Transaction Query creates a column UNDO_SQL. The SQL text in this field is the logical opposite of the DML operation performed by the transaction shown. The code from this field can usually reverse original transaction within reason (e.g. a SQL_UNDO INSERT operation would be unlikely to insert a row back at the same ROWID from which it was deleted). As a general rule, Oracle Flashback Transaction Query is used in conjunction with an Oracle Flashback Version Query that provides transaction IDs.

```
SELECT operation, start_scn, commit_scn, logon_user
  FROM flashback_transaction_query
    WHERE xid = HEXTORAW('09000900A9010000');

OPERATION    START_SCN COMMIT_SCN LOGON_USER
------------ --------- ---------- ------------
UNKNOWN         393394     393463 OCPGURU
BEGIN           393394     393463 OCPGURU
```

The following statement uses Oracle Flashback Version Query as a subquery to associate each row version with the LOGON_USER responsible for the row data change.

```
SELECT xid, logon_user
  FROM flashback_transaction_query
    WHERE xid IN (
      SELECT versions_xid
      FROM employees VERSIONS BETWEEN TIMESTAMP
        TO_TIMESTAMP('29-MAR-12 11.40.00 PM',
                     'DD-MON-YY HH:MI:SS AM') AND
        TO_TIMESTAMP('29-MAR-12 11.56.00 PM',
                     'DD-MON-YY HH:MI:SS AM')
       );
```

Recover tables to a point in time with the Flashback Table feature

The Flashback Table feature uses information in the undo tablespace to revert a table to an earlier point in time. When a Flashback Table operation occurs, new rows are deleted and old rows are reinserted.

To use the Flashback Table feature on one or more tables, use the FLASHBACK TABLE SQL statement with a target time or SCN. You need the following privileges to use the Flashback Table feature:

- You must have the FLASHBACK ANY TABLE system privilege or the FLASHBACK object privilege on the table.
- You must have SELECT, INSERT, DELETE, and ALTER privileges on the table.
- To flash back a table to a restore point, you must have the SELECT ANY DICTIONARY or FLASHBACK ANY TABLE system privilege or the SELECT_CATALOG_ROLE role.

For an object to be eligible to be flashed back, the following prerequisites must be met:

- The object must not be included the following categories: tables that are part of a cluster, materialized views, Advanced Queuing (AQ) tables, static data dictionary tables, system tables, remote tables, object tables, nested tables, or individual table partitions or subpartitions.
- The structure of the table must not have been changed between the current time and the target flash back time.
- Row movement must be enabled on the table.
- The undo data in the undo tablespace must extend far enough back in time to satisfy the flashback target time or SCN.

To perform a flashback table operation:

1. Identify the current SCN of the database. This will provide you the information needed to reverse the flashback operation later if you wish.

```
SELECT current_scn
FROM   V$database;
```

2. Identify the time, SCN, or restore point to which you want to return the table.

3. Ensure that enough undo data exists to rewind the table to the specified target.

```
SELECT name, value/60 MINUTES_RETAINED
FROM   v$parameter
WHERE  name = 'undo_retention';
```

4. Ensure that row movement is enabled for all objects that you are rewinding with Flashback Table.

```
ALTER TABLE table_name ENABLE ROW MOVEMENT;
```

5. Determine whether the table that you intend to flash back has dependencies on other tables. If dependencies exist, then decide whether to flash back these tables as well.

6. Execute a FLASHBACK TABLE statement for the objects that you want to flash back. It's possible to flashback to an SCN number or a timestamp value:

```
FLASHBACK TABLE employees
TO SCN 123456;


FLASHBACK TABLE employees
TO TIMESTAMP TO_TIMESTAMP('2012-05-16 08:30:00', 'YYYY-MM-DD
HH:MI:SS');
```

Back-out transactions using Flashback Transaction

You can use the DBMS_FLASHBACK.TRANSACTION_BACKOUT procedure to roll back a transaction and its dependent transactions while the database remains online. Transaction backout uses undo data to create and execute the compensating transactions to return the affected data to its original state. TRANSACTION_BACKOUT does not commit the DML operations that it performs as part of transaction backout. However, it does hold all the required locks on rows and tables in the right form to prevent other dependencies from entering the system. To make the transaction backout permanent, you must explicitly commit the transaction.

In order to configure a database for the Oracle Flashback Transaction Query feature, the database must be running in ARCHIVELOG mode. In addition, the database administrator must enable supplemental logging.

```
ALTER DATABASE ADD SUPPLEMENTAL LOG DATA;
```

To perform Oracle Flashback Query operations, the administrator must grant appropriate privileges to the user who will be performing them. For Oracle Flashback Query, the administrator can do either of the following:

- To allow access to specific objects during queries, grant FLASHBACK and SELECT privileges on those objects.
- To allow queries on all tables, grant the FLASHBACK ANY TABLE privilege.

For Oracle Flashback Transaction Query, the administrator will need to grant the SELECT ANY TRANSACTION privilege. To allow execution of undo SQL code retrieved by an Oracle Flashback Transaction, the administrator will need to grant: SELECT, UPDATE, DELETE, and INSERT privileges for the appropriate tables. Finally, the administrator will need to grant the user EXECUTE privileges on the DBMS_FLASHBACK Package.

Dependent Transactions
When you are tolling back a given transaction, there may be one or more dependant transactions. A dependent transaction is related by either a write-after-write (WAW) relationship, in which a transaction modifies the same data that was changed by the target transaction, or a Primary Key Constraint relationship, in which a transaction re-inserts the same primary key value that was deleted by the target transaction.

Backout Options

There are four options to TRANSACTION_BACKOUT. You're almost certain to see a question referencing this information on the test. The four options determine how the backout operation will handle any transactions that are dependent on the one being backed out:

- **CASCADE** -- Backs out specified transactions and all dependent transactions in reverse-order (children are backed out before parents are backed out).
- **NOCASCADE** -- This is the default option. It assumes there are no dependent transactions. If a dependent transaction exists, it will cause an error.
- **NOCASCADE_FORCE** -- Backs out specified transactions. If there are any dependent transactions, they are ignored. The server executes undo SQL statements for specified transactions in the reverse order of commit times.
- **NONCONFLICT_ONLY** -- Backs out changes to non-conflicting rows of the specified transactions.

Diagnosability Enhancements

Setup Automatic Diagnostic Repository

As mentioned earlier regarding the 11G changes to the Oracle flexible architecture, 11G has introduced the concept of the Automatic Diagnostic Repository (ADR). The ADR is a directory structure for diagnostic files such as traces, dumps, the alert log, health monitor reports, and more. The directory structure supports multiple instances and multiple Oracle products. Each instance of each product will store diagnostic data underneath its own home directory within the ADR. ADR provides a unified directory structure along with consistent diagnostic data formats across products and instances. This plus a unified set of tools enables diagnostic data to be correlated and analyzed across multiple Oracle products.

DIAGNOSTIC_DEST parameter
Because all diagnostic data, including the alert log, is stored in the ADR, the initialization parameters BACKGROUND_DUMP_DEST and USER_DUMP_DEST have been deprecated. They have been replaced by the initialization parameter DIAGNOSTIC_DEST. The DIAGNOSTIC_DEST parameter identifies the directory which serves as the ADR Base location.

ADR Locations
The V$DIAG_INFO view lists all the important ADR locations for the current Oracle database instance. It also provides the number of active problems and incidents and the tracefiles for the current instance.

- **ADR Base** -- Path of ADR base
- **ADR Home** -- Path of ADR home for the current database instance
- **Diag Trace** -- Location of background process trace files, server process trace files, SQL trace files, and the text-formatted version of the alert log
- **Diag Alert** -- Location of the XML-formatted version of the alert log
- **Default Trace** -- File Path to the trace file for the current session
- **Diag Incident** -- File path for incident packages
- **Diag Cdump** -- Equivalent to cdump. Location for core dump files.
- **Health Monitor** -- Location for health monitor output.

```
SELECT name, value
FROM V$DIAG_INFO;

NAME                  VALUE
--------------------- -----------------------------------------
Diag Enabled          TRUE
ADR Base              /u01/oracle
ADR Home              /u01/oracle/diag/rdbms/orclbi/orclbi
Diag Trace            /u01/oracle/diag/rdbms/orclbi/orclbi/trace
Diag Alert            /u01/oracle/diag/rdbms/orclbi/orclbi/alert
Diag Incident         /u01/oracle/diag/rdbms/orclbi/orclbi/incident
Diag Cdump            /u01/oracle/diag/rdbms/orclbi/orclbi/cdump
Health Monitor        /u01/oracle/diag/rdbms/orclbi/orclbi/hm
Default Trace File    /u01/oracle/diag/rdbms/orclbi/orclbi/trace/
                        orcl_ora_22459.trc
Active Problem Count  8
Active Incident Count 20
```

Use Support Workbench

Oracle Configuration Manager

The Support Workbench uses Oracle Configuration Manager (OCM) to upload diagnostic data to Oracle Support Services. If Oracle Configuration Manager is not installed or properly configured, the upload may fail. If this happens, a message is displayed with a request that you upload the file manually. You can upload manually through Oracle MetaLink.

Problems vs. Incidents

The fault diagnosability infrastructure in Oracle 11G introduces two concepts for the Oracle Database: problems and incidents. A problem is defined as a critical error in the database. Critical errors manifest as internal errors, such as ORA-00600, ORA-07445, or ORA-04031. Problems are tracked in the ADR using a problem key, which is a text string that describes the problem.

An incident is defined as a single occurrence of a problem. When a problem occurs multiple times, an incident is created for each occurrence. Oracle timestamps the incidents and tracks them in the ADR. Incidents are identified by a numeric incident ID, which is unique within the ADR. Each incident in the database generates the following actions:

- An entry is made in the alert log.
- An incident alert is sent to Oracle Enterprise Manager.
- Diagnostic data about the incident is stored in the form of dump files.
- One or more incident dumps are stored in the ADR in a subdirectory created for that incident.

Flood Control

A single problem could generate hundreds of incidents in a short period of time. If every action generated dumps as described above, this would generate a huge amount of diagnostic data. That much data would not aid diagnosis, would consume significant space in the ADR and could possibly slow down the process of diagnosing and resolving the problem. Oracle applies a flood control mechanism to incident generation to prevent this from happening. After certain thresholds are reached, incidents become flood-controlled. A flood-controlled incident generates an alert log entry and is recorded in the ADR, but does not generate incident dumps.

Threshold levels for incident flood control are predetermined and cannot be changed. They are defined as follows:

- After five incidents occur for the same problem key in one hour, subsequent incidents for this problem key are flood-controlled.
- After 25 incidents occur for the same problem key in one day, subsequent incidents for this problem key are flood-controlled.
- After 50 incidents for the same problem key occur in one hour, or 250 incidents for the same problem key occur in one day, subsequent incidents for the problem key are not recorded at all in the ADR. The database will write a message to the alert log indicating that no further incidents will be recorded.

The Automatic Diagnostic Repository has two distinct retention policies for incidents that determine how long data will be kept on disk from the time of the incident. The incident metadata retention policy determines how long the ADR will retain the metadata on incidents. It defaults to one year. The incident files and dumps retention policy sets the time that dump files will be kept. It is one month by default.

Incident Packaging Service

An incident package is a collection of metadata stored in the Automatic Diagnostic Repository which points to diagnostic data files and other files both related to a given incident. When creating a package, you select one or more problems to add to the package. The Support Workbench then adds associated problem information, incident information, and diagnostic files to the package. By default only the first and last three incidents for each problem are added to the package. Any incidents that are over 90 days old will not be included. After the package is created, you can add one or more external files, remove selected files, or edit selected files in the package to remove sensitive data. Only the package metadata is modified when performing any of these actions. When you are ready to upload the information to Oracle Support, you create a zip file that contains all the files referenced by the package metadata and upload the zip file through Oracle Configuration Manager. The Incident packaging service (IPS) is the tool which performs all of these steps. Because all diagnostic data in the ADR relating to a critical error are tagged with the incident number, the incident packaging service identifies them automatically and adds them to the zip file.

ADRCI

The Automatic Diagnostic Repository Command Interpreter (ADRCI) is a command-line utility that is part of the Oracle 11G fault diagnosability infrastructure. ADRCI's primary functions include:

- Viewing diagnostic data in the Automatic Diagnostic Repository.
- Viewing Health Monitor reports.
- Packaging incident and problem information for Oracle Support.

Diagnostic data viewable from within ADRCI includes incident and problem descriptions, trace files, dumps, health monitor reports, alert log entries, and more. ADRCI can be used in interactive mode or within scripts. ADRCI can also execute scripts of ADRCI commands just as SQL*Plus can execute scripts of SQL and PL/SQL commands. There is no login to ADRCI -- it is secured by OS-level file permissions only.

ADRCI HOMEPATH

An ADR home is the root directory for all diagnostic data for a particular instance of a given Oracle product or component. All ADR homes share the same hierarchical directory structure that starts at the ADR_BASE directory. Some ADRCI commands can work with multiple ADR homes simultaneously while others require that a single ADR home be set within ADRCI before issuing the command. The current ADRCI homepath determines the ADR homes that are searched for diagnostic data when an ADRCI command is issued. It does so by pointing to a specific directory within the ADR base hierarchy. When pointed to a single ADR home directory, that ADR home is the only current ADR home. If the homepath points to a higher directory, all ADR homes that are below the directory that is pointed to become current. The ADR homepath is null by default when ADRCI starts, which means that all the ADR homes beneath the ADR_BASE are current. The SHOW HOME and SHOW HOMEPATH commands display the current ADR homes. The SET HOMEPATH command sets the homepath to a specific directory.

Alert Log

Starting with Oracle 11g, the alert log is written as both an XML-formatted file and as a plain text file. You can view either format with any text editor. Alternately, you can use ADRCI to view the XML-formatted alert log with the XML tags stripped. By default, ADRCI displays the alert log in your default editor. You can use the SET EDITOR command to change the editor used by ADRCI.

Trace Files

You can use ADRCI to view the names of trace files that are currently in the ADR. You can view the names of all trace files, or a filtered subset of names. ADRCI has commands to obtain a list of trace files whose file name matches a search string, exist in a particular directory, pertain to a particular incident, or a combination of these. The SHOW TRACEFILE command displays a list of the files in the trace directory and in all incident directories under the current ADR home.

Show Incident

You can use the ADRCI SHOW INCIDENT command to display information about open incidents. For each incident, the incident ID, problem key, and incident creation time are shown. If the ADRCI homepath includes multiple current ADR homes, the report displays incidents from all of them.

```
SHOW INCIDENT

ADR Home =
/u03/app/oracle/product/11.1.0/db_2/log/diag/rdbms/orcl11g/orcl11g:
*************************************************************************
********
INCIDENT_ID  PROBLEM_KEY     CREATE_TIME
-----------  --------------  ----------------------------------
4218         ORA 603         2011-03-18 21:35:49.322161 -07:00
4219         ORA 600 [4134]  2011-03-20 21:35:47.862114 -07:00
4224         ORA 600 [4138]  2011-04-01 21:35:25.012579 -07:00
3 rows fetched
```

The following are variations on the SHOW INCIDENT command:

```
SHOW INCIDENT -MODE BRIEF
SHOW INCIDENT -MODE DETAIL
SHOW INCIDENT -MODE DETAIL -P "INCIDENT_ID=1681"
```

Packaging Incidents with ADRCI

Packaging incidents is a three-step process:

1. Create a logical incident package.
2. Add diagnostic information to the incident package
3. Generate the physical incident package

You can use either Oracle Enterprise manager or ADRCI to perform incident packaging. Using ADRCI, the initial logical incident package is created with the IPS CREATE PACKAGE command. There are several variants of this command depending on what metadata you want added to the package. For example:

- **IPS CREATE PACKAGE INCIDENT incident_number** will create a package with metadata referencing ADR data for the specified incident number.
- **IPS CREATE PACKAGE PROBLEM problem_ID** will create a package and include diagnostic information for incidents that reference the specified problem ID.
- **IPS CREATE PACKAGE PROBLEMKEY "problem_key"** will create a package with diagnostic information for incidents that reference the specified problem key.
- **IPS CREATE PACKAGE SECONDS** sec will create a package and include diagnostic information for all incidents that occurred from sec seconds ago until now.

- **IPS CREATE PACKAGE** with no additional information will create an empty package. You will need to add all incident data or files manually.

Once a package has been created (empty or not), you can add additional diagnostic information to it. You can add all diagnostic information for a particular incident, or individual named files within the ADR. To add an incident to an existing package, you would use the following command: **IPS ADD INCIDENT incident_number PACKAGE package_number**. To add a file, you would use the command: **IPS ADD FILE filespec PACKAGE package_number**. The file specification must be a fully qualified file name including the path. Only files that are within the ADR base directory hierarchy may be added.

Once the logical package has been created and any additional diagnostic data added, you create a physical package in the form of a zip file. The following commands issued from within ADRCI will generate incident packages:

- **IPS GENERATE PACKAGE package_number IN path** -- This generates a complete physical package in the designated path as a zip file.
- **IPS GENERATE PACKAGE 5 IN /home/george/oracle_support** -- This creates a physical package in the directory /home/george/oracle_support from logical package number 5:
- **IPS GENERATE PACKAGE package_number IN path INCREMENTAL** – This will generate an incremental package. An incremental package will contain only the incidents that have occurred since the last package generation.

Run health checks

The Health Monitor framework is new with Oracle 11G. Health Monitor is part of the Database Fault Diagnosability Infrastructure and is designed for running diagnostic checks on the database. Health Monitor checks examine various layers and components of the database. Checks can detect file corruptions, physical and logical block corruptions, undo and redo corruptions, data dictionary corruptions, and more. The health checks generate findings reports and often recommendations for resolving problems. Health Monitor stores all findings, recommendations, and other information in the Automatic Diagnostic Repository. Health checks can be initiated reactively or manually.

- Reactive health checks are run automatically in response to a critical error.
- Manual health checks are run manually by the DBA using either the DBMS_HM PL/SQL package or the Enterprise Manager interface.

There are two modes for running health checks, DB-online and DB-offline:

- **DB-online** mode means the check can be run while the database is open or mounted.
- **DB-offline** mode means the check can be run when the instance is available but the database itself is in nomount mode.

All of the health checks can be run in DB-online mode. Only the Redo Integrity Check and the DB Structure Integrity Check can be used in DB-offline mode. The available Health Monitor checks are:

- **DB Structure Integrity Check** —- Verifies the integrity of database files and reports failures if these files are inaccessible, corrupt or inconsistent.
- **Data Block Integrity Check** —- Detects disk image block corruptions such as checksum failures, head/tail mismatch, and logical inconsistencies within the block. This check does not detect inter-block or inter-segment corruption.
- **Redo Integrity Check** —- Scans the contents of the redo log for accessibility and corruption, as well as the archive logs, if available.
- **Undo Segment Integrity Check** —- Finds logical undo corruptions. If it locates an undo corruption, it uses PMON and SMON to try to recover the corrupted transaction.
- **Transaction Integrity Check** —- This is identical to the Undo Segment Integrity Check except that it checks a single specific transaction.
- **Dictionary Integrity Check** —- Examines the integrity of core dictionary objects, such as tab$ and col$.

DBMS_HM Package

You can run health checks manually using either Oracle Enterprise manager or the DBMS_HM package. The DBMS_HM package has a procedure called RUN_CHECK that is used for running a health check. To call RUN_CHECK, supply the name of the check and a name for the run, as follows:

```
BEGIN
  DBMS_HM.RUN_CHECK('Dictionary Integrity Check',
'di_check');
END;
```

The available heath checks can be found in the V$HM_CHECK view. You can obtain a list of health check names with the following query:

```
SELECT name
FROM   v$hm_check
WHERE  internal_check='N';

NAME
--------------------------------
DB Structure Integrity Check
Data Block Integrity Check
Redo Integrity Check
Transaction Integrity Check
Undo Segment Integrity Check
Dictionary Integrity Check
```

Most health checks have input parameters. The parameter names and descriptions are available in the V$HM_CHECK_PARAM view. Some of the parameters are mandatory and others are optional. When optional parameters are omitted, the default values are used. You can display parameter information for all health checks with the following query:

```
SELECT c.name check_name, p.name parameter_name,
       p.type, p.default_value, p.description
FROM   v$hm_check_param p, v$hm_check c
WHERE  p.check_id = c.id
AND    c.internal_check = 'N'
ORDER BY c.name;
```

You pass input parameters to the input_params argument of DBMS_HM.RUN_CHECK as name/value pairs separated by semicolons (;). The following example passes the transaction ID as a parameter to the Transaction Integrity Check:

```
BEGIN
  DBMS_HM.RUN_CHECK (
  check_name => 'Transaction Integrity Check',
  run_name => 'hm_run',
  input_params => 'TXN_ID=6.23.1')
END;
```

Using the Data Recovery Advisor

Overview of Data Recovery Advisor

Functions of the DRA

Oracle's Data Recovery Advisor is a data corruption repair function integrated with Support Workbench, database health checks and RMAN. It can display data corruption problems, assess their extent and impact, recommend repair options, and automate the repair process. In the context of Data Recovery Advisor, a health check is a diagnostic procedure run by the Health Monitor to assess the state of the database or its components. Health checks are invoked reactively when an error occurs and can also be invoked manually.

Failures

A failure is a persistent data corruption detected by a health check. They are usually detected reactively when a database operation encounters corrupted data and generates an error. This will automatically invoke a health check in the database. The check will search the database for failures related to the error and record any findings in the Automatic Diagnostic Repository. Data Recovery Advisor can generate repair advice and repair failures only after failures have been detected by the database and stored in the ADR. Data Recovery Advisor can report on and repair failures such as inaccessible files, physical and logical block corruptions, and I/O failures. All failures are assigned a priority: CRITICAL, HIGH, or LOW, and a status of OPEN or CLOSED.

- **CRITICAL** priority failures require immediate attention because they make the whole database unavailable. Typically, critical failures bring down the instance and are diagnosed during the subsequent startup.
- **HIGH** priority failures make a database partially unavailable or unrecoverable, and usually have to be repaired in a reasonably short time.
- **LOW** priority indicates that failures can be ignored until more important failures are fixed.

Repairs

Data Recovery Advisor allows you to view repair options. Repairs might involve the use of block media recovery, datafile media recovery, or Oracle Flashback Database. In general, Data Recovery Advisor presents both automated and manual repair options. If appropriate, you can choose an automated repair option in order to perform a repair. In an automated repair, Data Recovery Advisor performs the repair, verifies the repair success, and closes the relevant failures.

Repairing data failures using Data Recovery Advisor

The recommended workflow for repairing data failures from RMAN is to run the following commands in sequence during an RMAN session: LIST FAILURE to display failures, ADVISE FAILURE to display repair options, and REPAIR FAILURE to fix the failures.

LIST FAILURE

The LIST FAILURE command displays failures against which you can run the ADVISE FAILURE and REPAIR FAILURE commands.

```
RMAN> LIST FAILURE;
List of Database Failures
=========================
Failure ID Priority Status  Time Detected Summary
---------- -------- ------- ------------- -------
274        HIGH     OPEN    12-APR-11     One or more non-system
                                          datafiles are missing
329        HIGH     OPEN    12-APR-11     Datafile 1:
                                          '/u01/oradata/prod/
                                           system01.dbf'
                                          contains one or more
                                          corrupt blocks
```

ADVISE FAILURE

Use the ADVISE FAILURE command to display repair options for the specified failures. This command prints a summary of the failures identified by the Data Recovery Advisor and implicitly closes all open failures that are already fixed. The ADVISE FAILURE command indicates the repair strategy that Data Recovery Advisor considers optimal for a given set of failures. Data Recovery Advisor verifies repair feasibility before proposing a repair strategy. For example, it will check that all backups and archived redo log files needed for media recovery are available. It can generate both manual and automated repair options.

```
RMAN> ADVISE FAILURE;
List of Database Failures
=========================
Failure ID Priority Status  Time Detected Summary
---------- -------- ------- ------------- -------
274        HIGH     OPEN    12-APR-11     One or more non-system
                                          datafiles are missing
329        HIGH     OPEN    12-APR-11     Datafile 1:
                                          '/u01/oradata/prod/
                                           system01.dbf'
                                          contains one or more
                                          corrupt blocks

analyzing automatic repair options; this may take some time
using channel ORA_DISK_1
analyzing automatic repair options complete

Mandatory Manual Actions
========================
no manual actions available

Optional Manual Actions
=======================
1. If file /u01/oradata/prod/data01.dbf was unintentionally renamed
or moved, restore it

Automated Repair Options
========================
Option Repair Description
------ ------------------
   1     Restore and recover datafile 31; Perform block
        media recovery of block 43481 in file 1

Strategy: The repair includes complete media recovery with no data
loss
Repair script:
/u01/oracle/log/diag/rdbms/prod/prod/hm/reco_740113269.hm
```

CHANGE FAILURE

The CHANGE FAILURE command allows you to change the failure priority from HIGH to LOW or the reverse. You cannot change to or from CRITICAL priority.

```
RMAN> CHANGE FAILURE 3 PRIORITY LOW;
```

REPAIR FAILURE

The REPAIR FAILURE command is used to repair database failures identified by the Data Recovery Advisor. The target database instance must be started, it must be a single-instance database and cannot be a physical standby database. It is important that at most one RMAN session is running the REPAIR FAILURE command. The only exception is REPAIR FAILURE ... PREVIEW, which is permitted in concurrent RMAN sessions. To perform an automated repair, the Data Recovery Advisor may require specific backups and archived redo logs. If the files are not available, then the recovery will not be possible. Data Recovery Advisor consolidates repairs whenever possible so that a single repair can fix multiple failures. If one has not yet been issued in the current RMAN session, REPAIR FAILURE performs an implicit ADVISE FAILURE. RMAN always verifies that failures are still relevant and automatically closes failures that have already been repaired. After executing a repair, RMAN reevaluates all open failures on the chance that some of them may also have been fixed.

Perform proactive health check of the database

VALIDATE DATABASE

The VALIDATE DATABASE command validates all datafiles and control files, checking for corrupt blocks and missing files. If the database is currently using a server parameter file, then RMAN validates the file as well. By default, the VALIDATE command checks for physical corruption only. In a physical corruption, the database does not recognize the block at all. In a logical corruption, the contents of the block are logically inconsistent. You can specify CHECK LOGICAL to check for logical corruption. RMAN populates the V$DATABASE_ BLOCK_CORRUPTION view with its findings. Block corruptions can be divided into interblock corruption and intrablock corruption. In intrablock corruption, the corruption occurs within the block itself and can be either physical or logical corruption. In interblock corruption, the corruption occurs between blocks and can only be logical corruption. The VALIDATE command has the ability to check for intrablock corruptions only.

Health Monitor

Health Monitor provides two ways to run health checks proactively:

1. Using the DBMS_HM PL/SQL package. The DBMS_HM procedure for running a health check is called RUN_CHECK. To call RUN_CHECK, supply the name of the check and a name for the run:

   ```
   BEGIN
   DBMS_HM.RUN_CHECK('Dictionary Integrity Check',
                     'proactive_check');
   END;
   ```

2. Using the Enterprise Manager interface, found on the Checkers subpage of the Advisor Central page

Security: New Features

Configure the password file to use case sensitive passwords

Changes to Oracle Passwords

Oracle Database has added several enhancements to password security in 11G. Among them, you now have the following new features:

- The ability to locate standard accounts using default passwords.
- Enforced case sensitivity for database accounts by default.
- A password complexity verification function.
- Stronger password hashing algorithm.

Locating accounts with default passwords

In Oracle Database 11g, most of the default accounts are locked and have their passwords expired at database creation. However, if you have upgraded from an earlier release, there may be unlocked user accounts such as HR, OE, and SCOTT that are not locked and have default passwords. To improve database security, the passwords on these accounts should be changed. Failing to do so can make your database vulnerable to attacks. To find both locked and unlocked accounts that use default passwords, query the DBA_USERS_WITH_DEFPWD view from an account with SYSDBA privileges.

```
SELECT d.username, u.account_status
FROM DBA_USERS_WITH_DEFPWD d, DBA_USERS u
WHERE d.username = u.username;

USERNAME  ACCOUNT_STATUS
--------- ---------------------------
SCOTT     EXPIRED & LOCKED
```

Case-sensitive Passwords

New with Oracle 11G, user account passwords are case sensitive by default. You can alter this behavior using the SEC_CASE_SENSITIVE_LOGON initialization parameter. Only users with the ALTER SYSTEM privilege can alter the value of this parameter. Set it to

TRUE to enable case sensitivity or FALSE to disable case sensitivity. Oracle strongly recommends that you leave case sensitivity in passwords enabled.

Passwords were not case sensitive in previous releases of Oracle Database. If you import user accounts from a previous release into Oracle 11G, the passwords in these accounts remain case insensitive until the user changes his or her password from within 11G. This is also the case if you upgrade from an earlier release of Oracle to 11G. When the password of a user account from the previous release is changed, it will become case sensitive (assuming that SEC_CASE_SENSITIVE_LOGON is set to TRUE). You can find users who have case sensitive or case insensitive passwords by querying the DBA_USERS view. The new PASSWORD_VERSIONS column in this view indicates the release in which the password was created.

```
SELECT USERNAME, PASSWORD_VERSIONS FROM DBA_USERS;

USERNAME                   PASSWORD_VERSIONS
-------------------        -----------------
SMITH                      10G 11G
RICHARDS                   10G 11G
HARVEY                     11G
ROONEY                     10G
```

The passwords for accounts SMITH, and RICHARDS were originally created in Release 10g and were then reset in Release 11g. Their passwords, assuming case sensitivity has been enabled, are now case sensitive, as is the password for HARVEY, which was originally created in 11G. However, the account for ROONEY is still using the Release 10g standard, so it is case insensitive.

The account passwords in the Oracle password file will also be case-sensitive by default. You can control the case-sensitivity of the password file by using the IGNORECASE parameter when creating the password file with orapwd. By default, IGNORECASE is set to N, which means that passwords are treated as case-sensitive. To create a password file that is not case-sensitive, use the parameter ignorecase=y as below:

```
orapwd file=orapw entries=100 ignorecase=y
```

Encrypt a tablespace

It is possible to encrypt any permanent tablespace to protect sensitive data. Tablespace encryption is transparent to database users and your applications. Encrypted tablespaces are designed protect your data from unauthorized access by means other than through the database. This would include events such as someone getting hold of backup tapes of your database. Encrypted tablespaces also protect data from users who try to access database files directly through the operating system. When a tablespace is encrypted, all tablespace blocks are encrypted. All segment types are supported for encryption, including tables, clusters, indexes, LOBs, table and index partitions, and so on. To maximize security, data from an encrypted tablespace is automatically encrypted when written to the undo tablespace, to the redo logs, and to any temporary tablespace. There is no disk space overhead for encrypting a tablespace. The following statement creates an encrypted tablespace with the default encryption algorithm:

```
CREATE TABLESPACE secure_ts
DATAFILE '/u02/app/oracle/oradata/orcl11g/secure01.dbf'
SIZE 200M
ENCRYPTION
DEFAULT STORAGE(ENCRYPT);
```

Oracle Wallet

Tablespace encryption uses the transparent data encryption feature of Oracle Database. This feature requires that you create an Oracle Wallet to store the master encryption key for the database. The wallet must be open before you can create the encrypted tablespace and before you can store or retrieve encrypted data. When you open the wallet, it is available to all sessions. It remains open until you explicitly close it or until the database is shut down.

Encryption Algorithms

Transparent data encryption supports industry-standard encryption algorithms, including the following: 3DES168, AES128, AES192, AES256. The encryption key length is implied by the algorithm name. For example, the AES128 algorithm uses 128-bit keys. You specify the algorithm to use when you create the tablespace, and different tablespaces in the same database can use different algorithms. While longer key lengths theoretically provide greater security, there is a trade-off in CPU overhead. AES128 is the default encryption algorithm.

Restrictions

- You cannot encrypt an existing tablespace with an ALTER TABLESPACE statement.
- Encrypted tablespaces are subject to restrictions when transporting to another database.
- When recovering a database with encrypted tablespaces you must open the Oracle wallet that contains the encryption key after database mount and before database open, so the recovery process can decrypt data blocks and redo.

Configure fined grained access to network services

Network Services

The Oracle database contains a set of PL/SQL utility packages, such as UTL_TCP, UTL_SMTP, UTL_MAIL, UTL_HTTP, and UTL_INADDR, which are designed to enable database users to access network services from within the database. In a default database installation, these packages are created with EXECUTE privileges granted to PUBLIC users. Prior to Oracle 11G, this meant that any user with access to an Oracle account also gained access to all of these network services. This release enhances the security of these packages by allowing database administrators the ability to restrict access to these packages.

Creating Access Control Lists

To configure fine-grained access to external network services, you create an access control list (ACL), which is stored in Oracle XML DB. It's possible to create the access control list by using Oracle XML DB itself, or by using the DBMS_NETWORK_ACL_ADMIN and DBMS_NETWORK_ACL_UTILITY PL/SQL packages.

To create the access control list by using the DBMS_NETWORK_ACL_ADMIN package, follow these steps:

1. Create the Access Control List and Its Privilege Definitions via the DBMS_NETWORK_ACL_ADMIN.CREATE_ACL procedure.

```
BEGIN
DBMS_NETWORK_ACL_ADMIN.CREATE_ACL (
acl          => 'file_name.xml',
description => 'file description',
principal    => 'user_or_role',
is_grant     => TRUE|FALSE,
privilege    => 'connect|resolve',
start_date   => null|timestamp_with_time_zone,
end_date     => null|timestamp_with_time_zone);
END;
```

- **acl** -- a name for the access control list XML file.
- **description** -- a brief description of the purpose of this file.
- **principal** -- the initial user account or role being granted or denied permissions.
- **is_grant** -- either TRUE or FALSE, to indicate whether the privilege is to be granted or denied
- **privilege** -- either connect or resolve. Connect grants permission to connect to a network service. Resolve grants the user permission to resolve a network host name or an IP address.
- **start_date** --(Optional) starting date that the entry will be valid.
- **end_date** --(Optional) ending date that the entry will be valid.

2. Add additional users or roles to the access control list, or grant additional privileges to one user or role, via the DBMS_NETWORK_ACL_ADMIN.ADD_PRIVILEGE procedure. The matching parameters that exist in ADD_PRIVILEGE and CREATE_ACL have the same meaning. The only new parameter is "position", which sets the precedence for multiple users or roles.

```
BEGIN
DBMS_NETWORK_ACL_ADMIN.ADD_PRIVILEGE (
  acl => 'file_name.xml',
  principal => 'user_or_role',
  is_grant => TRUE|FALSE,
  privilege => 'connect|resolve',
  position => null|value,
  start_date => null|timestamp_with_time_zone,
  end_date => null|timestamp_with_time_zone);
END;
```

3. Assign the access control list to one or more network host computers using the DBMS_NETWORK_ACL_ADMIN.ASSIGN_ACL procedure. Only one access control list can be assigned to any host computer, domain, or IP subnet, and if specified, the TCP port range. When you assign a new access control list to a network target, Oracle Database unassigns the previous access control list that was assigned to the same target.

```
BEGIN
  DBMS_NETWORK_ACL_ADMIN.ASSIGN_ACL (
  acl => 'file_name.xml',
  host => 'network_host',
  lower_port => null|port_number,
  upper_port => null|port_number);
END;
```

- **acl** --the name of the access control list XML file to assign to the network host.
- **host** -- the network host to which this access control list will be assigned. This setting can be a name or IP address of the network host, or you can enter localhost.
- **lower_port** -- (Optional) For TCP connections, enter the lower boundary of the port range. Use this setting for the connect privilege only; omit it for the resolve privilege. The default is null, which means that there is no port restriction (that is, the ACL applies to all ports).
- **upper_port** -- (Optional) For TCP connections, enter the upper boundary of the port range. Use this setting for connect privileges only; omit it for resolve privileges. The default is null, which means that there is no port restriction (that is, the ACL applies to all ports).

ABOUT THE AUTHOR

Matthew Morris is an Oracle Database Administrator and Developer currently employed as a Database Engineer with Computer Sciences Corporation. Matthew has worked with the Oracle database since 1996 when he worked in the RDBMS support team for Oracle Support Services. Employed with Oracle for over eleven years in support and development positions, Matthew was an early adopter of the Oracle Certified Professional program. He was one of the first one hundred Oracle Certified Database Administrators (version 7.3) and in the first hundred to become an Oracle Certified Forms Developer. In the years since, he has upgraded his Database Administrator certification for releases 8i, 9i, 10G and 11G, and added the Application Express Expert certification. Outside of Oracle, he has CompTIA certifications in Linux+ and Security+.

12979282R00093

Printed in Great Britain
by Amazon.co.uk, Ltd.,
Marston Gate.